Gladiators Vs Zombies

By Sean-Michael Argo

DEDICATIONS

George Romero, the man who brought us the zombies.

Andy Whitfield, for showing us what heroes are made of.

Author's Forward:

    The title says it all… Zombies are the ultimate bad guys, and we love pitting them against all sorts of heroes. I have been a zombie fan for years, and fascinated by Roman Gladiators for a lifetime, so it was only natural that I eventually write a mash-up story. In this tale of blood and honor we are given glimpses of a wide variety of characters that inhabit this imagined ancient world. In this book you will encounter much in the way of Latin terminology and a wide variety of historical references. It is important to keep in mind that this book is fiction, and not meant to serve in any way as an accurate depiction of gladiators, historical events, or religious beliefs. While I have made attempts to present a story that has an authentic feel to it, I have taken a great many creative liberties. I do hope you enjoy reading this as much as I enjoyed writing it.

THE GOLEM

The rabbi Ezekiel looked out across
the battlements towards the vast Roman
army, his gaze moving across the
earthworks and tents of the amassed
legions, falling finally upon the massive
wooden platform the Romans had
constructed. It stood at a great height
and had been growing day by day for
months. Soon the edge of the platform
would reach the gates of Masada, the
mountain fortress upon which the last
remnants of the Jewish revolt waited to
make their last stand.

While he watched workers hammering
and lashing, swarming over the platform
like so many ants, his mind traveled back
to the beginning of the revolt. So
brightly had their courage shone, as
radiant as their swords and spears,
though not yet tested against the
strength of the Legions. In the early
days of the struggle, the Jewish rebels
had been victorious in skirmishes with
the local garrisons, and the fires of
revolt had since spread across the
region. Victory and freedom seemed within
their grasp, yet all too soon it was
snatched away as the Roman legions
marched across the region, bringing
reprisal with them.

Ezekiel turned his back on the army
below and looked upon the people of
Masada, all of whom had gathered at the
temple to hear his words and receive his
judgment. The men were haggard and war-

weary, the long months of siege having taken its toll on both their numbers and their spirit. The women stood silent and stoic, their hearts as hard as their faces. The children did not play or sing, only gazed with hollow eyes empty of mirth or innocence.

"Our time on this earth is done, my flock. Soon the Romans will be at our gates, and we all know what the Pax Romana will mean for us. The men will be killed where they stand. Our women will be defiled, many unto death. Our children will be taken as slaves and raised to love other gods." intoned the rabbi as he stepped down from the battlements and walked among his people. "We cannot allow this terrible fate to befall us."

"What to you propose, rabbi?" spoke Kohath, one of the few veteran warriors who had taken up a sword to join the revolt. "There is no ground left to defend, nor is there any hope for escape. Is it the dishonor of suicide that you seek to set upon us?"

Ezekiel knelt to pick up a fistful of sand from the ground and held it above his head so all could see. "I will use the letters, and I will breathe life into a man born of sand and clay. A golem." As the rabbi spoke, a murmur went through the assembly, some backing away in terror, others whispering in excitement.

"You speak of ancient things Ezekiel, dark magics that were outlawed by King Solomon ages ago." Kohath argued as he stood firm, his hands crossed over his chest.

"Do not fear! It is with this man of clay that we shall bring terror and defeat upon the Romans. We shall set our hands against them even after death, for no grave can hold the wrath of God. All one must do is look out upon the armies set against us to see that we are doomed. But we are His chosen people, and shall not pass so meekly from this world."

"Dishonor or darkness," spat Kohath as he turned to look out at the Roman legions camped below. "They are poor choices old friend. Though if death extends in all directions, I'll walk the path that brings the Romans down. Darkness it is then."

"A holy choice. Surely you will all be rewarded in heaven for the righteous retribution you will now bring to the Roman dogs."

That night, Ezekiel and two of his disciples mixed blessed water with sand, shaped the form of a man from cold clay stored in the damp darkness of the inner temple, and set themselves to the task of creating a golem. The rabbi and his disciples sung prayers and spoke the words as they crafted the man of clay. They burned incense over the body and sent their god the sacrifice of the camp's last goat, thrown on a ritual fire so the smoke could carry their prayers skyward. At the end of the ritual, Ezekiel took his carving tool and wrote the sacred words upon the forehead of the golem. Upon the last stroke of the last letter, the eyes of the clay man shuddered and opened.

The people of Masada gathered around the temple as commanded by Ezekiel, and he brought them down to the inner sanctuary one at a time. Each person was led down the shallow steps, held arm in arm by the two disciples as Ezekiel prayed over them all. They were brought before the man of clay, who was now bound firmly in the center of the temple. The golem's teeth gnashed as he moaned like a starving man, struggling against his bonds. Each person was presented to the golem, some more willingly than others, and the creature would bite the hand offered to it. Then Ezekiel would again bless the person and anoint them with oil, saying "With this sacrifice of flesh we call upon your wrath, Mighty God."

Dawn had broken across the sky by the time everyone in camp had been bitten, including Ezekiel and his disciples. Everyone had armed themselves as best they could, some with sword and shield, others simply with sticks and rocks. They shared a common meal, using their wounded hands to break bread as a tribe one last time. Then, as dawn gave way to full morning, they began to die.

THE CENTURION

Centurion Cyprian Africanus awakened in a cold sweat, heart pounding in his chest and pugio dagger in his hand. Dreams, just dreams, he told himself. He had been in the underworld, fleeing from hordes of dead souls. Many soldiers of his own cohort had been at his heels, most of whom in the waking world yet lived. Wine, he needed wine. Being a man of the sword, he had developed a thirst for drink, though he kept it within as much moderation as any man could. It calmed his nerves unlike any other balm. Ever since his tour of duty in the hard north against the savage blue painted men, nothing else would suffice.

He stood up from his cot, crossed the room, and poured himself a hefty measure. Quaffing the bitter wine and savoring the taste, he focused on the warmth of the liquid as it spread through his body. Calm now soldier, it was just a dream. As the heady potency of the wine cleared the fog of sleep from his mind, he dropped to the ground and began his daily exercise regiment, followed shortly by a stretching routine. With his body work finished, he toweled the sweat from his body while draining a cup of water from the basin, then began strapping on his armor. This was his way on all mornings.

Cyprian emerged from his tent and fastened his centurion's helmet as a messenger approached him. "Centurion

Cyprian Africanus, your century has been chosen to lead the vanguard. We assault the mountain within the hour." With that, the messenger went on his way, no doubt to deliver orders to the rest of the cohort. Cyprian simply grunted in assent and nodded, then walked with a leader's purpose into the encampment of his soldiers, bellowing for muster.

Within minutes the soldiers stood in perfect formation, the light of dawn glinting off of polished armor, their spear-tips shining like so many stars. One hundred of the hardest men in all the legions of Rome, he thought to himself as he looked them over. We have walked across the broken swords of countless armies, each man a veteran of a dozen wars. It was an honor to lead the vanguard, one that Cyprian and his men had earned. Let these Jewish rebels hide behind their mountain, and we shall root them out.

The assault platform was a vast construct, a testament to the engineering power of a modern military. To see it made the centurion's heartbeat quicken with pride. He'd watched as it underwent various stages of construction for a grueling, boring score of months, never giving it a second glance. Yet now, before him it stood, glorious and mighty. The century assembled at the base of the platform and then, as the drummer beat out a marching rhythm, the formation began to move up its massive length.

The sound of war-horns was in his

ears as Cyprian marched alongside his soldiers. The platform was wide enough for ten legionaries to march shoulder to shoulder, a hundred boots pounding up the structure towards the gates of Masada. With their voices, they bellowed out a deep marching chant. With their hands they beat spears against shields on every fourth step, emitting the terrible cadence that had struck such fear into enemies of wars past. The whole of the encampment was watching from below, and the relief columns cheered as they watched their comrades marching upwards.

As the column neared the gates, Cyprian began to grow wary. Archers should be defending the walls, he thought, and by now they should hear challenge from the soldiers waiting to defend the gate once it fell. Silence was all that met the Romans as they drew near. "Shields!" barked the centurion, and his men responded, bringing their expertly crafted shields above their heads in tortoise formation. In an instant, the column was completely protected from above, creating a roof through which arrow and stone could nary penetrate. The shields had been smeared in siege oil, a recipe of Cyprian's own divining, designed to deny purchase to burning pitches or any other unsavory liquids hurled down on them by the defenders. And yet today, nothing fell.

"Battering ram!" Cyprian commanded as the column reached the gate doors unhindered. A ripple went through the column as disciplined men stepped aside to allow another group of soldiers, carrying a thick wooden pole, to move through the ranks. The iron-tipped pole looked like a giant arrow covered in rope handles, its wooden shaft darkened from much use. The cohort had used this very ram several times in battle. Cyprian had heard legionaries around the campfire refer to it as 'The Bitch.' It had earned its name, he thought, and soon in the hands of twelve strong men, it upheld the name once again as its point drove open the gate in eleven skillful strikes. The crossbeam splintered to bits, and the weighty doors swung open.

"Take the center!" yelled the centurion as the column poured into the mountain fortress. The soldiers rushed into the center of the fortress and began forming the square formation, their shields locking together as the men stood side by side. His gaze swept across the empty compound, the hackles on his neck rising for still no enemy harassed them. No defenders met their entrance, and in minutes, the entire century had entered the fortress while the relief column waited at the base of the platform many yards below.

"Steady lads! Let them come to us." Cyprian intoned as his forward assault began to lose its momentum. The marching cadence had ground to a halt, and the soldiers stood silent. And then they heard the moaning. At first it was a lone voice, then a cacophony of voices, all calling out in a confusing drone. "Steady!" cried the centurion as he moved out from the square, a bold habit that had earned him the derision of his fellow centurion officers and yet won him the total loyalty of his own men.

He walked several yards forward, searching for some sign of this wailing enemy. Soon his eyes fell upon the first of them. Cyprian could tell by the man's clothing that he was a rabbi, though his clothes were torn and bloody, and the man's demeanor was strange. His skin was ashen grey in color and he moved at an awkward pace, almost like a blind man searching for purchase. The rabbi's pale head suddenly turned toward the centurion, his lips drawing back in a snarl as he let out a bestial scream. Cyprian took a step back. Something was shaken in his soul, some primitive fear gripped his heart, and he felt in an instant as if he could barely stand.

The rabbi moved towards the centurion, his gait now some shuffling sprint, screaming and gnashing his teeth as he went. Cyprian fell back quickly and rejoined the ranks as the lone enemy came onwards. The rabbi lurched into the open ground of the main plaza where the rest of the men could now see him. They too felt the disgusting terror, Cyprian could see it, that same bowel emptying primal fear. The rabbi paused, for the briefest of moments, his eyes burning yellow and hateful. Then the rest of the defenders revealed themselves.

Across the fortress screaming voices erupted as dozens of the Jewish rebels entered open ground. All of them had wounds on their hands, blood on their clothing, the same gnashing teeth and deadly pallor as the rabbi. Cyprian would have sworn the rabbi looked directly at him as the creature screamed and the entire rebel force surged towards the soldiers.

"Spears!" cried the centurion, and a flight of pilium spears flew out from the square formation. Many of the rebels were impaled, and yet all of them kept charging, as if unaffected by the spears piercing their bodies. Seeing the enemy only pause, the centurion barked "Second throw!" and the men deeper inside the square hurled their spears, all to similar effect. The enemy would not be slowed, it seemed, and were upon them at once. Cyprian freed his gladius from its scabbard and yelled furiously for the men to draw sword alongside him.

The perfect military formation was a flash of iron as one hundred of Rome's finest raised their swords and prepared for the oncoming attack. The first wave of rebels crashed into their lines, slamming themselves into the shield wall with reckless abandon. In mere moments, Cyprian could see that these creatures were far from mortal men. Killing blows would barely slow them down; some of the rebels took mortal wounds several times over and only kept coming with crazed determination. The centurion saw scrabbling hands tear shields away and begin tearing at the men with hands and teeth. In a moment of pure terror, Cyprian saw that some of the men were literally being eaten, as if the rebels were ravenous beasts.

After several moments of bloody combat, Cyprian lost sight of the greater struggle as the rabbi himself rushed the centurion. His mouth running with blood and meat, the rabbi looked less like a beast and more like a monster of legend. Centurion Cyprian Africanus was not a superstitious man; however he had fought in enough wars with the blue people to assume that whatever horror he saw before him was real enough, and he raised his weapons against it. The two met in a bone-crunching embrace, the rabbi slamming against Cyprian's shield with inhuman force. The centurion bent his knees and torqued to the side, sending the rabbi-creature to the ground with a shattered arm. Cyprian recovered and brought his shield back into position just as the rabbi fell upon him again, grasping the shield and wresting it from his grasp, all the while seemingly impervious to the many thrusts from the centurion's shortsword.

The rabbi-creature forced his hands under the centurion's armor, causing the Roman to lose his balance and fall to the ground. Cyprian nearly vomited with fear as the rabbi-creature crawled atop him and brought its mouth down to his face. The centurion managed to get his sword up

in time to prevent the rabbi-creature
from biting him, though only barely, and
the blood-crusted teeth chomped down on
the iron blade instead. Cyprian lost his
grasp on the sword and screamed in pain
as the rabbi-creature's hands began
tearing and beating at his armor, so hard
that he could barely remain conscious.

Cyprian's hand fell to his hip and
his hand closed around his pugio. The
centurion managed to get his hand around
the throat of the rabbi-creature and
before it could react, he plunged his
dagger into the thing's temple. To both
his relief and surprise, the creature
began twitching violently and collapsed
upon him. Not wanting to be caught on the
ground, Cyprian threw the body off of
him, recovered his gladius, and sprang to
his feet.

"Romans! To me! The heads! Take
their heads!" Cyprian shouted as he flew
into combat with another rebel, cleaving
its head from its shoulders as if to lend
credence to his bold words. The century
had been halved in number already,
though, as a testament to the Roman war-
machine, the remaining soldiers fought
back with focused discipline and
determination. Through the carnage they
reformed the square, fighting back-to-
back and shoulder-to-shoulder against the
rebel-creatures. When one man would tire
or fall, another would step forward to
take his place.

The relief column had begun pounding
up the ramp once battle was joined and

arrived within minutes to aide in the struggle. Shouts of the creatures' weaknesses were called from Cyprian's century, and the fresh soldiers quickly helped turn the tide. The last of the creatures were put to the sword and soon there were none left standing. With the skill of a seasoned leader, Cyprian steadied his pounding heart, recaptured his breath, and took command of the relief column, instructing the men to search the rest of the compound at once. The order had already been given to kill, defile, or enslave every living person in the compound, so no stone was left unturned.

Cyprian chose two of his century's best surviving men to accompany him into the temple. The three Romans found the door unbarred, which was unusual for these curious zealots of Judea. Typically great treasures of gold and spice could be found within their temples, and, after the hardest fight of his life, the centurion intended to claim it. They descended the shallow stairs into the center of the temple, and there they found the golem.

To the eyes of a Roman soldier, the golem looked like any other man, though with a strange tattoo on his forehead in the language of the Judean tribes. While his men ransacked the temple, Cyprian knelt down, bringing himself to eye level with the tattooed man. He looked into the shackled man's eyes and recognized the same feral hatred and hunger as he had in

the rabbi and the other rebel-creatures.
The centurion was again filled with a
fearsome disgust. And still, the tattoo
intrigued him. As such, the centurion did
what any good Roman soldier would do: he
cut the man-creature's head off and
claimed it for himself.

THE LANISTA

Lanista Atticus Laeca was troubled, though, being a man of perfect pragmatism, it was not the moaning severed head on his desk that gave him concern as much as the accounting ledger in his hands. It was simple mathematics; there was more coin going out than coin coming in. The cost of maintaining Ludus Laeca was greater than the reward of his house's participation in the games. A shame that, he thought to himself as he poured a measure of wine into his goblet and walked to the window of his small office. I have but two gladiators who have the potential to one day be champions: Bricius and Agathias, he thought, though neither have been granted a primus or even a secundus match in the games. And true though Heraus the Boar was a brutal killer and undefeated, he was too fearsome a man to ever win the love of the crowd.

Atticus looked out through the open window into the training yard of his modest ludus. On the sun-baked sand, nearly two dozen men trained in the fighting arts, sweat pouring off of their well-muscled bodies as they struggled to keep pace with each other. The sound of wooden practice swords connecting with shield and flesh was a constant staccato. Once, when he was a younger man and fresh to the world of games, that sound had sent the lanista's heart to racing. His grandfather had founded Ludus Laeca upon his return from nearly twenty years in the Legion. A decorated veteran, the lanista's grandfather had used his entire lifetime of careful savings to make his dream a reality. The old man had several barbarian slaves he'd captured in his last campaign, and he'd built his initial victories in the arena with their blood. From there, it was a gradual growth from his grandfather's small ludus of five gladiators to the proud Ludus Laeca of today, boasting nearly twenty-five mighty warriors of the arena.

"From tiny seeds grow mighty trees," his grandfather had said, adopting some barbarian phrase he'd heard on campaign. The old man had commissioned a sign saying such and put it on display in the training yard. Atticus supposed that, for some of the men down there, a saying from their own people could provide some small comfort. Atticus had first grown up in the ludus as the grandson of the lanista. When his father took over, he became the son of the lanista and now, forefathers all passed, he was the proud lanista himself. His father before him had been an ambitious man, possessed of a love of coin matched only by his love of the games, a love he passed to his son.

While his grandfather had focused on the training and perfection of single gladiators, preferring a quality over quantity approach to the games, the lanista's father, Felix, had dreamt quite differently. Felix would buy far more slaves and would train them only in the basics of battle before hurling them into the arena. He would insist to his son that there were men born for glory and men born for slaughter. He said that as a lanista, it was his calling to tell one man from the other. "Raise up the champions, throw the rest into the bloodbath." House Laeca swiftly gained wealth and reputation for being a purveyor of bulk bloodshed, and won the majority of the contracts for the mock battles that required death on a grand scale.

Sadly for Atticus, when the ludus passed into his hands the tastes of the Roman mob had shifted away from rivers of blood and returned to a desire for feats of skill. No longer did the crowd wish to see dozens of men hacked to pieces in wild melees, or to see slaves and criminals armed only with daggers be slaughtered by quality gladiators. The Roman audience now craved matched pairs of champions, skilled gladiators fighting grand duels for personal glory and the love of the crowd. Rome wanted the gladiators of his grandfather, thought Atticus, not the arena fodder of his father's time.

Lanista Atticus had done his best to stay relevant in the games. He had taken the few men of quality who remained in his stable and began crafting them into what he believed were true champions, though due to the reputation of the ludus, Atticus was still unable to secure position in any of the larger games, even for them. Truly all of his men were capable warriors and all trained fiercely. They were each gladiators in their own right; however none were to the standard of the great games of the Coliseum, and as such, fought in the smaller arenas spread throughout Rome and its provinces. Heraus, an older man and the last surviving gladiator of Felix's stock, fought almost exclusively in the bloody pits of the noxii: the black market arenas in which condemned criminals and slaves were forced to fight.

This simply would not do. Atticus cared about his ludus and took his life as a lanista seriously. He must find a way to rise up, to elevate Ludus Laeca once more. At this thought, he turned from the window and looked at the severed head on his desk. Its skin was a deathly pallor; the ragged wound at the base of its neck had been carefully wrapped in scented cloth and its yellowed eyes burned with an unsettling vitality. According to the centurion from whom Atticus had purchased this thing, the tattoo which appeared on its head meant 'life' in the language of the Hebrews.

Several days past, Atticus had been called upon by Centurion Cyprian Africanus, a well-known veteran of the Legio VII. The soldier had sent word ahead to the ludus that his arrival was eminent, asking for audience with the lanista for the purpose of a business transaction. Atticus knew that the seventh legion had recently returned from a campaign in Judea, though, given their billet in the distant city of Capua, he could not imagine the centurion's reason for making the journey to Rome itself. Possibly the soldier intended to sell the lanista several slaves for the pits, though the tribes of Judea were not especially known for breeding the kinds of warriors that made good gladiators. Atticus was quite curious as to what business the soldier might bring.

Centurion Africanus was granted audience. The cunning lanista made sure to ply the soldier with food, drink, and small talk before inquiring as to the nature of the visit. Atticus had long been a shrewd judge of character in men; it was his job to see the champions or beasts lying quiet in their souls, to stoke the fires that would craft them into fine warriors. In the centurion, Atticus saw a hardened soldier, a patriot of Rome, and yet he saw a fear in the man too, some sense of dread or disgust rippling just beneath the surface.

Soon, after several cups of wine, the centurion began to tell his tale. Atticus listened quietly and intently as the soldier spoke of his century's assault on the mountain fortress of Masada. The lanista shifted in his seat, mesmerized by the horror written on the centurion's face as he recounted the desperate battle with the creatures. After he'd spoken of the tattooed man's head, the centurion paused, as if returning his thoughts to the present moment with some difficulty, then he reached into his satchel and produced the very head he'd cut from the golem's shoulders.

Atticus leapt from his seat in shock as the severed head opened its eyes, its mouth working against the gag which bound its jaws shut. As the lanista recovered his composure and re-took his seat, the centurion told the remainder of his tale. Cyprian had heard campfire stories about the golems of the Jews, magical creatures that were men who were made of clay, then bestowed with life by the Jew who created them. They were servants, but, according to the Judeans, were cursed creatures who brought only sorrow upon those around them. He'd always dismissed it as a tall tale, typical amongst soldiers on campaign and yet, when he set his eyes upon the still living severed head, he knew there had to be some truth in the stories.

So curious was he of this supernatural marvel, Cyprian had bound the golem's jaws and taken the head as a prize. It was then that Cyprian leaned forward, his gaze transfixing Atticus. "It was the bites Lanista, the bites transformed them," he had said. "Many of the men who were killed in battle soon rose again and attacked us as if they too were on the side of the rebels. Of my hundred men, only eighteen left the field alive, and a score of them had been bitten by the creatures, some more than once. Many soldiers in the relief column were bitten as well. We thought little of these bites, as wounds in battle are common to us, so we bound them with healing herbs and continued in our duties."

Atticus poured himself another strong measure of wine and gulped it down in two swallows as the centurion finished his grisly tale. The soldier's face was pale as a shade while he described the madness of that evening's events. "I cannot be sure when it began exactly, but the men who had been bitten fell grievously ill and expired during the night. Most fell unnoticed in their tents, though some perished in the medicae." He continued as he glanced down at the golem's head resting on the table. "Within moments of death, they… I do not know how else to say it… returned to life, just like the men killed in battle. Though they were like this golem creature, ravenous beasts that seemed to care only for consuming the flesh of men."

"In the depths of the night, these creatures, these golems, moved among the camp, slaughtering the men. We are men of the seventh legion and veterans of many wars, and so we rallied as we always have. Word had spread of our battle on the mountain, and, once we knew it our own men who were attacking us, we were swift to mobilize. It was a long and bloody night lanista, and many more men were bitten and transformed before we realized that the source of transformation was the bites themselves. Our losses were tremendous from the massacre in the night, then grew larger with the following day's executions of those survivors who were bitten. In a day, the legion lost two thirds of its strength." Cyprian stared into his goblet, swirling the last of the wine around, losing himself for a moment in his awful memories before speaking again. "Legio VII is to be disbanded within a month's time. Most of the soldiers will be transferred to other cohorts, and the few men of my own century, including myself, will be retired. Which brings me to my business with you, lanista."

Atticus was quickly brought out of his reverie, his thrilling conversation with Cyprian fading from his mind as a knocking came on his office door. "Enter." he said as he picked up the head and placed it in its box under his desk. Hesta, the Greek slave girl, opened the door bearing a small plate of food.

"Your midday meal, Dominus." she spoke softly, her head bowed, as she brought it to his table.

"Ah, yes, thank you." Atticus smiled, watching her with great scrutiny as she set the food on the desk and stood before him with her head bowed. The lanista felt a stirring in his loins as his eyes moved up and down her body. He knew the small group of slave girls in his household took turns bringing his midday meal; all of them knew that in the afternoons, his appetites tended to be for more than simple nourishment. Lanista Atticus Laeca had been a widower since his wife died giving birth to his daughter. A certain darkness had filled him then, and since that time, Atticus had chosen not to take a new wife. Instead he focused on the business of his ludus, and slaked his lust upon the supple flesh of his young slaves.

He could see the grim acceptance in Hesta's demeanor, and it cooled his desire. He was a kind man, and handsome enough, though he supposed he did use his slaves roughly when lust was upon him. A small matter, as the golem's low muffled moan brought him back to the business at hand. "You may take your leave," he said as he made a dismissive gesture. The visibly relieved girl walked quickly out of the office, gently shutting the door behind her.

Atticus opened the box and removed the head, placing it upon the desk next to his untouched food. The centurion had theorized that the bites from the golem's mouth would transform a living person into the undying cannibal creatures in Cyprian's tale. The lanista thought back to the height of his father's business, the days when coin flowed, even if glory and honor did not. If he could bring to the arenas of Rome a spectacle that was as much a marvel as it was a terror, his ludus would rise in both status and wealth. These golems, these creatures of myth made flesh, could be the answer he had been looking for.

Lanista Atticus Laeca walked down the narrow hallways of the slave pens with the box held snugly beneath his arm. His doctore, the trainer of his gladiators, had ordered the house guards to move five of the least promising slaves into a single cell. Far from the gladiator's holding pens, and originally designed as a disciplinary cell for unruly slaves, it was perfect for what Atticus intended. In the small room now crowded with slaves, the lanista removed the golem's head from the box and unbound the gag from it's mouth. With the aid of his guards and the doctore, he allowed the head to bite each of the terrified slaves on the shoulder. "Watch them closely," he told the guards, "and fetch me when they start to sicken." The guards nodded their assent, and, after several hours had passed, the lanista was summoned to return to the holding cell.

With a morbid curiosity, Atticus surveyed the five slaves through the bars of the cell. They were each severely weakened, barely holding onto the spark of life. Atticus ordered the guards to bring a stool and he sat himself down, watching in silence as the men perished before him. The deaths occurred at roughly the same time, only moments between each of them. Atticus took note of this. He sat in silence, watching the bodies, his heart thundering in his chest as he waited, hoping his expensive purchase of the golem's head had been worth the money. That centurion was going to be able to retire comfortably with the sum Atticus had paid, emptying the savings of the ludus in a single transaction. A small matter, thought Atticus, as the ludus was doomed to fail within the year at any rate. If this gamble did not pay off, it would not change the inevitable. If it did work, however, then fame and fortune would be his.

There on the floor, the first of the bodies began to twitch. The rest followed shortly. Soon the eyes of the dead men began to flutter and open. They moaned as they writhed, and Atticus recognized the burning hatred and hunger in their searching eyes. Rising to their feet, the men began grasping at Atticus and his guard through the bars. They hurled themselves against the barrier in a frenzy to get at the living men on the other side. The lanista smiled, congratulating himself on his forethought in reinforcing the cell prior to this demonstration. The bite marks on their shoulders were like slave brands, and at that moment, Atticus knew that it would be the symbol of his new breed of slaves. The lanista beamed with arrogance as he turned from the cell to return to the villa. His gamble had paid off and his blood was hot, so he went in search of Hesta, who, it seemed, had not escaped his lust today after all.

THE BESTIARIUS

Gedra closed his eyes, taking a deep breath as he clenched his quaking hand into a tight fist. The moans of his new opponents had been ceaseless since they had transformed, and rest had not come easily to him the night before. Now he stood before the closed arena gates, knowing that across the sun-baked sands, another gate withheld the golem creatures of his dominus. Golems, that is what Lanista Laeca had called them last night during the hero's feast, a traditional last supper for the men who would fight the next day. Gedra had no appetite during the meal, and, as he now prepared to enter the arena, he was thankful for the empty stomach, sickened as he was by his enemy.

Gedra had fought in the arena ten times in the two years since being trained as a gladiator. He was one of the bestiari, the beast fighters, and though often an outcast in the company of other gladiators, a certain respect was still paid unto him. Unlike the other gladiators, who trained to battle armed men, the bestiarius had been taught the art of killing ferocious beasts. Gedra had fought such creatures as exotic as the ostrich bird, with its powerful kicks and sharp talons, as well as creatures as common but deadly as lions and bears.

Often the animals were sick and starving by the time they were turned out into the arena, and Gedra's tactic was to wear them down until he could deliver a killing blow. He still had to give the crowd a good show though and as such, he would occasionally rush in to strike at the foe. As long as the blood flowed, the beasts roared, and Gedra conducted himself with poise and grace, the crowd howled with joy at the brutal spectacle.

His body was a latticework of scars, as even the best of tactics were incapable of saving his flesh from the claws, teeth, and talons of his opponents. While he had been schooled in the use of the spear and bow that were the common weapons of the bestiari, there were bouts in which the editor of the games would require Gedra to fight with other weapons. If the editor wanted to prolong the bout, or if he needed to satisfy a particularly bloodthirsty crowd, then Gedra would be forced to fight with sword and dagger, or sometimes a spiked cestus glove. It was in these close quarters battles that Gedra would emerge from the struggle nearly as slashed and bloody as his defeated foe.

Today's battle seemed to be set up more traditionally, and Gedra was armed with a short stabbing spear and a small oval shield. It was not the long spear of the beast hunts, but a short spear with a wide blade that could slash or stab. The bestiarius had used such weapons in bouts with larger animals, once against a bear and once against a massive boar. The gladiator was confident, though wary of his new opponents. It was the way a bestiarius should be.

With the grinding of heavy hinges, the gates to the arena opened and Gedra stepped out onto the sand. He held his arms up in salutation to the crowd, who returned his pose with cheers. Though the bestiarius was an outcast among his fellow gladiators, the crowd often cheered loudly for the beast hunter, as he represented a symbolic mastery of man over beast. Still, this same crowd that cheered his entrance into the arena now would cheer just as loud should be torn limb from limb. The people grew silent as the gates on the other side of the arena began to creak open in turn.

The editor had prepared the crowd before the games began, speaking to them of the grand new beasts being offered to the arena by Ludus Laeca. Now everyone waited eagerly to see what fresh horror emerged from the darkness. At first there was only a low moan, but then one of the golems shuffled out onto the dusty arena floor. He was dressed in tattered clothing, and on his shoulder was the ragged bite wound that was reflected in the cloth banner Lanista Laeca had hung over the gate. The crowd remained silent, confused that a man walked into the arena and not a beast. Gedra knew better, for he had heard the moaning the night before, and knew the man he now faced had once been a slave in the lanista's household.

The golem groaned again as its yellowed eyes scanned the crowd,

staggering to the side for a moment as if
overwhelmed by the presence of so many
onlookers. From within the masses,
someone shouted "This is no beast!" as
the rest of the crowd began to follow
suit, echoing their dissatisfactions.
Then, as if spurned on by the detractors,
the golem's gaze fell upon Gedra. From
within it's twisted mouth, the creature
let out a bestial scream and began its
move towards the gladiator.

At first, the gait of the creature
was more like a shuffle, but within
moments became something between a walk
and a run. It was graceless and wild.
Gedra began to return the approach,
hoping to make quick work of this sad
creature. He knew not what strange blight
the wound on the creature's shoulder
signified, though he felt sorry for the
man. Clearly he was suffering from some
disease or drug the lanista had forced
upon him to make him more like a beast.
Gedra was sickened by the whole affair,
the honor of his position as bestiarius
was being slighted by calling this poor
man a beast.

Without breaking stride, Gedra
deflected the man's outstretched arms and
drove his spear into the man's mid-
section, twisting the point of the spear
as he stepped to the side. As he did, the
spear rent apart the man's belly and the
golem's putrefying guts spilled out into
the arena. Gedra recovered and stepped
back, his shield sinking back into
position before him, his gory spear

resting against it. Typically when he performed this maneuver, the beast would bellow and collapse, ending the fight as it bled out upon the sand. Gedra watched and waited for similar results.

The golem staggered several steps away from the pile of guts on the arena floor, but it did not fall. The crowd grew deathly silent and Gedra began to realize that he was in more peril than he'd realized. This man was not a man at all, but some manner of creature, indeed deserving of the name 'golem' given by the lanista, though the bestiarius still had no idea as to the word's meaning. The shredded golem screamed horribly once more and careened towards Gedra, heedless of the tremendous wound in its belly. The bestiarius backed away several steps and then lunged again, sinking his spear into the golem's chest.

This time, the creature only halted briefly, then pushed forward against the point of the spear as it continued its pursuit of the bestiarius. Gedra's grip on the spear loosened, the weapon ripped away as the golem twisted its torso in an attempt to get past the gladiator's shield. The crowd erupted in a combination of cheers and boos as the bestiarius took several hasty steps backwards from the creature, trying to regroup. The golem kept coming, uncaring of the spear jutting from its chest, its arms outstretched once more.

Gedra knew he could not keep retreating or he would lose the favor of the crowd and bring shame to his ludus. He had been trained to control the fight and to never let the beast gain the upper hand in determining where the battle moved. With no additional weapons, the gladiator waited until the beast was a few steps closer, then moved to the side as he delivered a crushing blow with his shield. The shaft of the spear snapped, and the creature's bottom jaw exploded in a spray of blood and bone. The crowd howled its delight as the creature fell to the ground.

Gedra let himself relax for the briefest of moments, the fight seemingly done, but suddenly the creature was again on the offensive. From the ground, the creature grabbed the gladiator's greave and began to haul itself up, using his leg. Gedra took a step back, but the creature's grasp held and it sank its teeth into his exposed thigh. Gedra had been bitten and clawed many times before, but there was something unusually terrifying about being bitten by a man. The creature wrenched its head back and forth and tore free a huge chunk of meat from the gladiator's leg, sending the man crashing to the ground.

Gedra screamed in pain and lost his grip on the shield as the creature batted it aside. The golem and the gladiator grappled for several moments, rolling around on the arena's sand floor until the creature bit down into Gedra's left hand. The gladiator yelled in pain and began punching the golem's face with his free hand, though no matter how many blows he landed, nothing seemed to slow the attacker. The creature began using its hands to tear at the flesh of the bestiari's belly, and, despite the punishing storm of fists, the golem was able to lend its teeth to the task.

Gedra's screams became whimpers as he continued to struggle against the creature, though once its hands slid into his belly through the holes torn by its teeth, the fight went entirely out of him. The bestiarius died to the sound of his guts being torn out and eaten by the golem, while the crowd looked on in stunned silence. Soon the golem stood up from the partially eaten gladiator and began staggering around the arena, wailing and looking at the crowd.

By this time, many people in the stands had vomited, others were too shocked to even do that. Not a sound could be heard save the moaning of the golem until the bestiarius stood up. The thing that was once Gedra looked out at the crowd and began moaning, staggering towards the people. It was then that a very satisfied Lanista Laeca gave the signal to the editor, who shouted for the arena tenders to recover the golems. From behind the gates, several men appeared carrying long poles with looped ropes fastened to the ends. Keeping a safe distance, the men wrapped the loops around the necks of the two golems and dragged them back into the darkness within the arena gates.

After a few moments of stunned silence, the editor erupted with delight, lauding Ludus Laeca for its incredible display. Soon the crowd followed suit, their cheers rising ever more deafening as they began to fully realize what they had just witnessed. Horrific, yes, but marvelous too. And so it was that the golem became the favorite opponent of gladiators in the arenas of Rome.

THE SECUTORES

Drust ran his hands across the tattooed skin of his arms, chest, and face, the ancient story of his people inked upon his living flesh. Violence had always been part of his people's way, as had beauty, for according to the tree-seers, these were the two forces that held together this world of mist. He was thankful today, as he often was, that he had been a warrior in his life before being enslaved as a gladiator. In his time he had seen plenty of slaves hacked to pieces in the arena having only first taken up the sword a scant few days prior. For Drust, as with many of his barbarian brethren, be they Celt or Gaul or Goth, the life of a gladiator was not that different from the life of a warrior.

Drust had been a skirmisher, conducting lightning raids against the Roman invaders who defended the outposts that stood before Hadrian's Wall. Small war parties, no more than a score of warriors, would gather in the dawn mists and harass the outposts. They would rush the walls, some hurling spears at the guards while others would toss lit torches in high arcs to land within the defenses. When good luck and good winds were with them, the torches would catch on and spread throughout the outpost. Then, while the Romans fought the fire, the skirmishers would scale the walls unmolested. Once over the walls, they would rampage through the outpost, each man following his own course, sowing chaos and death throughout the camp. Often the Romans would rally and begin to organize a defense, and it was then that the Picts would melt away into the forest, refusing to engage the Romans in the kind of stand-up fights at which the legions excelled.

These tactics worked well to slow Roman expansion into Pictish territory and prompted the Romans to build their massive wall. It was during one of these fiery raids that Drust fought Legionnaire Lucias Meridius and was bested by the Roman. Drust's life was spared, and the legionnaire sold the Pict to a slave trader on the other side of The Wall. The further south that Drust was taken, the more exotic he seemed to the covetous buyers. He was bought and sold several times before finding himself being trained as a gladiator in Ludus Laeca.

Being a man of callous pragmatism, Drust took to the life of a gladiator with the same tenacity with which he had once defended his homeland. The Picts typically fought with shield and spear, using their short swords as secondary weapons, though Drust had always excelled with a sword. As such, Lanista Laeca and the doctore trainer soon tapped him to be a Secutore style gladiator. Drust deeply disliked the unwieldy helmets gladiators were forced to wear, though after having his life saved several times in the arena by the helmet's protection, he learned to accept the sacrifice of vision and mobility.

Drust now stood on a small platform stationed just below the center of the arena. On the same platform stood two other secutores, both men of Ludus Laeca, though their names were unknown to the Pict. Drust kept few friends in the ludus, and apart from the old man Heraus, few knew much of him beyond his fearsome reputation in the arena. The previous lanista, Felix, had established Ludus Laeca as a house of mass battles and discount gladiators, and despite Lanista Laeca's attempts to change the house's reputation over the years, it was still largely regarded as such. Though perhaps the lanista no longer minded, as his golems had become the most spectacular craze in all of Rome.

The Pict thought back to the fate of the first man to fight the golems in the arena, Gedra the Bestiarius. So poorly did he die, and all for ignorance of how to kill the creatures, though certainly knowledge of their weakness was no guarantee of survival. Since the appetite for golem fights and carnage had reached a fever pitch in Rome, the Pict knew that anything could be waiting for he and the other gladiators in the arena. Thoughts of the terrible unknown steeled his nerves as the arena tenders began to pull the ropes attached to the platform. The gears turned and creaked as the wooden stage rose into the air, growing ever closer to the gateway hidden in the arena floor.

The three secutore on the platform stood silently, the harsh sunlight glinting off of their polished armor as the gates finally opened. The platform was raised flush with the arena floor, and the gladiators could now see what awaited them. Over a dozen of the golems had been released into the arena and were milling about the space, snapping and moaning at the jeering crowd above.

"If we stand together, we'll fare better," uttered the secutore to Drust's left. "Back to back, at least they will not be able to flank us."

Drust nodded in assent, but the other secutor shook his head and began to move away from them. "Do what you will brothers, I'll take my chances alone."

The sickly creatures in the arena noticed the three men in the center and began moving towards them. The lone secutor rushed out to meet the first of the golems, while Drust and his comrade stood their ground, standing back to back and slowly moving in a circle to cover all of the angles. The lone secutor bravely attacked the nearest golem, displaying his fighting skill as he used his shield to knock aside the golem's outstretched hands. While the golem reeled from the blow, the lone secutor brought his gladius around in a wide arc and swept the creature's head from its shoulders. As blood fountained upwards from the neck stump, the body collapsed, and the crowd roared its applause. The lone secutor took a step back and held his sword and shield high in a victory salute.

Drust tried not to show his distaste for the display. He hated the showmanship that was required of gladiators in the arena, preferring to do his butcher's work and return to his cell without pomp or circumstance, though as a slave this was not his choice to make. The lone secutor had struck first blood and was required by the rules of the arena to share this glory with the crowd. For the greater glory of Rome, scoffed Drust silently to himself. The other golems seemed to be shifting their attention to the lone secutor and his showman's display, and while that took pressure off of the other two gladiators, it was a mark against them if they stood idle while another took all the glory. So it was in the bloody protocols of the Coliseum.

"Moving right!" shouted the comrade secutor. Walking as one, Drust and the other gladiator took several steps to the right and engaged a golem that had been closing in. While his comrade sliced off one of the golem's hands, Drust darted forward and separated the golem's calf from its leg with his gladius as a wave of cheers erupted from the crowd. The golem continued to moan as it fell to the ground, bouncing off of Drust's shield as he deflected the falling body away. The comrade secutor drove the point of his sword into the back of the golem's skull, and after a spasm, it lay still.

Across the arena, the lone secutor was met with more cheers from the masses as he sprinted forward and shield-bashed a golem to the ground, stabbing downwards to finish the kill. While catching his breath, he noticed several more of the creatures closing in around him, so he quickly sprinted away from their grasping hands towards another lone golem. He knew he'd have to take them one at a time. The secutor tried his shield swipe move once again, though instead of it knocking the golem's hands away, the creature was able to get the first grasp on the shield. As it stumbled back from the force of the blow, the golem pulled the unwilling secutor along with it. The gladiator lost his balance and fell hard to his knee. Pressing down upon him, the creature pulled spastically back and forth on the shield, ripping it away just as the gladiator managed to bunch his legs beneath him. He sprang upwards and thrust his blade through the underside of the golem's sickly jaw. The point was rammed all the way through, reappearing at the top of the creature's skull in an explosion of blood and rotting brain matter.

The crowd went wild with shock and praise as the secutor pulled hard and drew the gladius from the golem while it collapsed to its knees and fell to the side. The gladiator made to recover his shield, but had to leap backwards as another golem swiped at him with its hands. The secutor opened a furrow in the creature's chest as he lashed out with his sword by instinct. The blow bought the gladiator enough space to turn and sprint away from the growing number of golems now chasing after him.

Meanwhile, Drust and his comrade secutor moved in a tight circle, each of them engaging a golem of their own. Drust was a measured and careful fighter, not prone to showboating or fancy moves. He fought as he drilled, with precise movements, relying upon speed and persistence to win his battles. He had won in the arena many times by wearing his opponent down with a constant barrage of attacks, and this battle was proving to be no different. With his shield, Drust protected himself from the grasping hands and tackle attempts of the golem while he lashed out with his gladius in repeated attempts to deliver a killing blow to the thing's head. The Pict struck again and again, the sword hacking out chunks of flesh and bone as it bit into the golem's neck, shoulders, and head. On the fifth blow, the Pict was able to sink his gladius into the temple of the golem. The thing twitched and fell to the ground in a heap as the Pict chanced a quick glance over his shoulder to see his comrade secutor thrust the point of his gladius into the eye socket of the golem he had been fighting.

A hiss went up from the crowd, and Drust turned to see the lone secutor limping away from the bodies of two more felled golems, his right thigh a ragged mess of bite marks. At least he still has his sword, thought Drust, as the Pict pivoted to deflect the awkward tackle of another golem, bringing his gladius up over his head and slamming it into the base of the golem's neck. His comrade secutor rushed to Drust's left and body checked another creature, then the two of them dispatched it with simultaneous strikes to its head. Before they had a chance to recover, another golem hurled itself at them, tackling Drust to the ground. His sword fell from his grasp, though he managed to keep the golem firmly on the other side of this shield as it clawed and snapped at his flesh.

"Lift your shield!" bellowed the comrade secutor. Drust grunted with the effort of pushing his shield upwards, lifting the golem with it. The comrade swung his gladius like a scythe and buried it halfway through the creature's skull, directly between its eyes and nose as the crowd roared again. The comrade bent to retrieve his weapon but found it was hopelessly stuck in the creature's head. With more golem's left to fight and no weapon in hand, he stepped back and began to unfasten his helmet. It would have to do. As Drust recovered to his feet, he deftly lopped off the arm of another charging golem, then knocked it to the ground with his shield and finished it with the point of his sword.

The two secutore stood back to back and continued to fight, Drust with his calculated barrage of attacks and his comrade secutor swinging his helmet as a bludgeon. In a matter of moments, they stood alone on the arena sands, save for the lone secutor who had by now turned into a golem himself. The man's body was large, even by gladiator standards, and he roared deeply as he charged towards them. Until now, the golems had not seemed inclined or capable of using weapons, and yet the secutor golem still grasped its sword, raising it as it ran awkwardly and powerfully forward.

"I'll go low and you go high," spoke Drust as the two gladiators stepped forward to engage their former brother. Drust snaked forward, keeping his legs bent and shifting his weight in a successful attempt to feint right. The golem clumsily swung its gladius downwards, its strike hitting the sand where Drust had been just moments before. The Pict lashed out with his gladius and severed the hamstring of the thing's right leg, then its left. As the creature sank to its knees, Drust's comrade secutor sprinted forward, putting all of his momentum behind a mighty blow with his helmet.

The golem's face shattered from the impact, painting Drust's shield in blood and bone chunks. The golem fell backwards from the force of the strike and did not move again. Drust and his comrade secutor raised their arms in victory, and Drust found himself screaming with exultation in spite of himself. It had been the greatest golem fight since they had been revealed in the arena, and though the glory of Rome meant nothing to the Pict, he took fierce pride in knowing that once again he had come face to face with death, and once again, he had overcome.

THE RETIARIUS

Octavian had long regretted the petty acts of thievery that had led to his condemnation and subsequent enslavement, though he could never bring himself to curse the gambling lust that drove him to steal. Even now, as he faced down death, his thoughts went towards his wager on the very bout he was about to fight. Octavian always betted on himself to win, for in his mind there was no reliable odds in the whim of the crowd, so loss of a bout might as well be death. Every time he went into the arena he would bet the whole of his coin on his own victory, and though he often won, his few losses had set him back to zero. He could not understand why any man would bet on anything but victory, and this thinking had cost him and won him fortunes many times over.

Today the odds seemed favorable and he was in high spirits. Octavian had shown an aptitude for showmanship, a gift of theatrics beyond those of even the famously cavalier Agathias, the hoplomachus, also a gladiator in House Laeca. Octavian had once been trained as a spear fighting hoplomachus, though his charisma was sufficient, so Lanista Laeca decided to shift the gladiator's focus. Octavian had been given net and trident and trained as a retiarius, the most dramatic showmen of all gladiators.

He had excelled as a retiarius, winning not only coin and glory, but also the love and adoration of the crowd. This was evidenced today as he strode into the arena, greeted by a cacophony of voices calling out praise. The Lanista Laeca had done his job well, expertly spinning the tale of Octavian's rise from condemned noxii to glory-laden gladiator, so he was well favored among the people. Though his victories were not as numerous as those of the likes of Bricius the murmillo, and though he was never featured in the primus, secundus, or even tertius bouts, his face was handsome, and the crowd responded to his presence.

Often, as with today's match, Octavian was put into the arena for provocatore bouts. He would battle other theatrically gifted gladiators, and they would dance, pose, and engage the crowd just as much as they would fight each other. The bouts remained at their core a battle of life and death, though they were clearly meant to be more of a spectacle than a display of martial prowess. Still, men did die, and more than a few had been slain upon Octavian's trident.

Octavian looked across the arena and saw his opponents, letting his eyes flow over them as he sized them up. Lanista Laeca has outdone himself this time, thought Octavian as he looked upon the three female golems arrayed against him. The lanista had discovered that highly trained fighters, like the gladiators, often maintained some rudimentary skills and instincts when they were turned into golems. More often than not, a fallen gladiator who was turned into a golem could still use weapons with some minimal skill. No golem would ever parry a strike, or attempt a feint, but some of them were quite capable of basic slashes and thrusts, even if their form was awkward and their speed reduced. The three golems before Octavian had clearly once been gladiatrix, the rare and much debated female counterparts to the gladiators of Rome. From the horrific wounds already present upon their bodies, Octavian guessed that they had been killed in some previous bout, but, judging from the still fresh look of their wounds, these gladiatrix could not have been transformed more than a few days ago. The editor called for a start to the bout, the chains binding the golem gladiatrix to the arena floor were unfastened, and the arena tenders rushed behind the closing gate as the golems began moving towards them.

Octavian took a moment to prime the waiting crowd. "If you are looking for a man to fill you, fair maidens, I, Octavian, have a tine for each of you!" He brandished his trident, smiling widely as his jape was received with laughter and applause. Two of the golem gladiatrix were armed with medium-sized oval shields and curved sickle swords in the Thracian gladiator style. Once carried the small buckler shield and long spear of the hoplomachus. With no strategy to speak of between the blood-thirsty gladiatrix, each careened towards Octavian at their own speed. Wanting to open the fight with plenty of flair, the retiarius bounded directly towards the golems. Then, as he neared them, he feinted right, drawing a clumsy slash from the gladiatrix on the far left. While she was over-extended from her missed strike, Octavian cast his net across her, pulling it tight and binding her firmly as he circled around behind her.

With his momentum behind him and his superior weight doing the work, Octavian pulled back on the net, allowing the golem to fall backwards to the ground. The retiarius then began running in the opposite direction of his opponents, dragging the bound golem in the net behind him. He pumped his legs hard, dragging the undead creature swiftly to the far edge of the arena, putting great distance between himself and the other two golems. He released the net and held his arms out to the crowd nearest him, allowing them a close look at the golem who thrashed wildly in her roped prison, firmly bound.

"Look, my friends! A beautiful mermaid is caught in my nets! Shall I make a bride of her? Or do we say more fish in the sea?" He called out to the crowd, who began applauding and chanting in reply, "More fish! More fish!"

Octavian bowed with a flourish and took up his trident, holding it aloft as he spun it in his hands to reverse the grip. Then, as the golem continued her struggle in the net, he drove the trident downwards, two of his weapon's three tines disappearing into the golem's watery eye sockets. By the time he pulled the trident from the fallen golem's face, he could see that the other two had closed the distance. They would soon be upon him. He had not expected them to be as swift as they were, having seen several golem fights from the gladiator holding pens near the arena, and had to bring his trident up in a hasty block as one brought its gladius in a wide arc towards him.

Octavian pushed aside the blade and swept the butt of his trident across the golem's face, knocking it to the side and sending it crashing into the other creature. The retiarius danced several steps backwards, then began strutting in a wide circle around the two tangled golems who thrashed and snapped at each other as they disentangled and regained their footing.

"You see how they hiss and argue? How lucky am I, a mere slave, to be desired by such beauties!" voiced Octavian as he took a moment to flex his muscles and strike a pose, smiling as he was met with more applause. The faster of the two golems, a redhead with half of her face missing, reached him and again slashed at him in a wide arc. The veteran gladiator ducked under the strike and planted his feet while executing a perfect lunge into the golem's mid-section. He lifted upon the trident, bracing the butt of the pole-arm against his foot, and used the golem's momentum to carry it up and over his head. He kept his grip firm on the trident, turning on his feet and twisting his torso to maintain control of the weapon as the golem slammed onto her back against the arena floor.

Unfortunately, upon impact, Octavian's trident had split in two. The fracture from the gladius block, he thought. In this grim realization, he released his grip on the now useless trident. Throwing his opponent overhead had always been his signature move in the arena, and this time it had cost him his weapon. But this was not a time to lose composure, he told himself, and quickly he turned to engage the golem that he knew would be coming up behind him. The gladiatrix made a clumsy thrust with her spear, which Octavian sidestepped, pirouetting on the balls of his feet to move outside her grasp. As he did, he set one hand on the shaft of her spear and with the other hand, delivered a bone crunching forearm strike to the golem's unarmored wrist.

The golem lost its grip on the weapon and careened forward as Octavian brought the spear into a guard position with a spinning flourish that brought cheers from the crowd. He sprang forward and thrust the spear into the creature's back, then pulled the weapon free as he danced in a circle around the golem, thrusting the point home several more times. The crowd went wild with this display, and Octavian bathed in their adoration. While Octavian raised his arms in a final salute to the crowd, the golem gladiatrix he had previously thrown overhead and impaled was rising behind him, trident tines still buried in her graying flesh. So focused on the showmanship of his last golem kill, neither Octavian nor the crowd seemed to see the danger growing just a few steps away. The golem gladiatrix stood wobbling for a moment, as if confused, its hands questing inquisitively around the broken shaft of the protruding trident, then ripped it free from its body.

A cry of horror went up from the crowd. Octavian turned just in time to block the trident with his forearm as the golem gladiatrix drove it down towards him in an overhead strike. The tines pierced through his arm in three places as he fell to his knees in pain. He screamed ferociously and punched the golem in the mid-section, knocking it back a pace, then swept its legs aside with his own. As it fell to the ground, Octavian, all theatrics forgotten, scrambled backwards and pulled at the trident stuck in the bone of his arm. The golem gladiatrix crawled toward him on all fours like a ravenous beast, finally leaping upon the wounded man. The retiarius frantically brought the trident up to defend himself, stabbing the golem in the neck, though to little effect. From his face, the golem tore a piece of flesh with its teeth, and they both fell prone on the sand. In a flash, the creature was atop the fallen gladiator, tearing out his throat with savage bites and clawing madly at his unarmored flesh.

The crowd that had so loved Octavian while he yet lived now cheered ever more loudly as he died. Within moments, he was transformed, and the arena tenders came to remove two golems from the blood-soaked arena floor.

THE MAIDEN

Hesta looked at herself in the mirror-like surface of the water basin. Despite her hard life, her face was still as beautiful as the day when she'd first been taken as a slave. The men of her city-state had risen against Roman rule, and the city had been engulfed in riots and reprisals. The local Roman garrison had crushed the dissenters swiftly, preventing the riots from turning into a full-blown revolution. As part of the reprisals levied upon the city, the Romans had taken slaves from the local population. She had heard in the camps that there was an official order given to take only known dissenters or their families, though, as with many such orders given throughout the empire, it amounted to wanton capture and enslavement.

She was a beautiful woman, and young, so she was valued above many others. The men were sent to labor camps, most of them to be shipped off to fill quotas on the vast building projects across the empire. Those men who were not fit for building were consigned to the mines, which for most of them was tantamount to a death sentence. For children it was much the same, with some few being held for duty as household slaves and work in stables, as children were known to have a natural aptitude for animal husbandry. Women were treated far less roughly though many would have gladly chosen the mines. The old or unattractive were sent to the sculls and kitchens, to cook and clean, or weave and craft if they'd the skill. The women who were of a younger age or possessed of particular beauty, and even some of the fairer men, were sold at a high price to brothels and to houses of wealthy Romans. For many Roman households, there was a certain unspoken status enjoyed by those whom owned beautiful slaves.

Hesta was such a beauty, no matter how she wished it were not so. As such a prized slave, she was not abused or raped in captivity, her virginity kept intact so she could command greater price upon being sold. She worked as a household slave to her dominus, the slaver who had contracted with the garrison to collect the levy. Over the following year, she had learned the art of silence and was grateful for the many comforts she knew so many others did not have. But she had also learned about the darker side of being purchased property. While her dominus was particularly concerned that Hesta and the other three young virgin slaves remain unspoiled, he had no such concern with the others in the house. A cruel man, he had forced Hesta and her slave-sisters to watch as the other women were brutalized by any man with coin to pay. The slaver insisted that the virgins know their place, and that they be prepared to give their future dominus pleasure when he took their maidenhead.

To demonstrate the cost of displeasuring their future masters, the dominus callously used and murdered one of the other women. It was at that moment Hesta vowed to herself and her gods that she would not die a slave.

Hesta remembered one afternoon, after her first year in the house, she was told to present herself before the dominus. When she arrived, the remaining virgin, Gorgo, was already attending him. Gorgo stood naked before the dominus and a newcomer who was introduced to her as Lanista Atticus Laeca.

"Disrobe, girl, and let us feast the eyes of our friend Lanista Laeca," said the dominus as he sipped his wine. Hesta did as she was told, her heart fluttered as she saw the look of appreciation and expectation in the eyes of Lanista Laeca.

"A feast indeed, Tiglath. You know my tastes well, old friend," smiled Lanista Laeca as he devoured the slave girl with his eyes.

"I suspect that a man in your profession is, like myself, wise in his judgment of flesh and the potential which lies hidden beneath appearances. Be it a fine fighting man to bleed for you in the arena, or an unspoiled woman in which to plunge yourself into!" boasted the dominus as he bit down on a greasy chunk of meat spitted upon his knife. Lanista Atticus Laeca nodded his agreement in silence, never taking his eyes away from Hesta, his gaze causing her bare skin to flush.

Hesta looked at her reflection now in the water basin, the memories coming to her in a flood. The lanista was soft-spoken and handsome enough, carrying himself with the confidence of a man accustomed to having power over others. He came to her on the first night in the villa above the ludus. Unlike the dominus and the cruel men that were his usual companions, the lanista was surprisingly gentle. But this would not last.

Hesta had only been a slave in House Laeca for a few months when the lanista's wife died in childbirth. And Atticus, as she had come to call him while they lay sweating in the darkness when his desire was spent, was a changed man from then on. He was deeply wounded by the death of his wife, whom all knew he loved dearly. "This great loss," he'd said "all for the meaningless birth of a worthless daughter." It was as if his soul began to grow dark that day, and soon he became a cruel, cold, and hardened man. The ludus had fallen on hard times financially, more so once the lanista lost his wife. He'd pulled away from most human contact, spending nearly all of his time in his office, brooding over accounts.

Lanista Laeca spared no love or time for his young daughter, leaving her to the care of his household. He was often lost in his own mind, in thoughts of the games and how to increase the flow of coin into his house. Outside of these few things, it seemed the only thing he paid attention to was his desire for Hesta,

which had grown considerably. Upon her
flesh, more than any other slave, he
would serve his lust. Over time, his
passions had grown darker alongside his
spirit, and his coupling with her grew
ever more abusive. Hesta often turned to
her prayers for comfort, finding so
little of it in the life she lived in
House Laeca. Such was his newfound
passion in humiliating her, that Atticus
would force her to attend him in the
ludus while his gladiators trained. He
would lead the slave girl down into the
empty pens while the men worked their
fighting skills above. Once, in the
madness of his passion, Hesta had chipped
a tooth on the cell bars as he forced her
to bite them while he took her.

Most of the gladiators hated the
lanista, and as they were all slaves of
the same dominus, many resolved to show
Hesta high regard and respect in spite of
him. Little did they know that doing so
only spurred Atticus to ever more deviant
acts. Such was the simple ignorance of
good men. The ludus had become a grim
place, more so now that the golems were
part of the games, and the men constantly
contemplated their looming deaths doing
battle against the undead creatures. For
many gladiators, the sight of the
beautiful slave girl was enough to keep
them going, seeing that some spark of
beauty still remained in the world.

Hesta knew this of the gladiators
and drew strength from them in return,
though it cost her dearly when Lanista

Laeca would notice her smiling at one of the warriors, or see her linger a moment longer than needed as she tended their bruises or gave them water. In their sad equilibrium, the men kept her spirit from breaking, and she kept them fighting. Perhaps Lanista Laeca knew of this and used it to his own advantage. For surely gladiators who fought bravely and clung to life while in the jaws of death were far more profitable than the slaughter of men without hope. She could not be sure if the lanista's mind went to such thoughts, but it mattered little so long as they all felt some measure of hope.

Her god was Dionysus, and she sought solace in her prayers to him. She kept her covenants and sometimes, in the darkness, with incense in the air and wine coursing through her veins, he would answer.

THE THRACIAN & DIMACHERI

Asur moved his arms back and forth as he bounced from one foot to the other, keeping his muscles warm and his heart pounding. This was just another bout, he told himself, one more contest of arms. He was trying to keep himself calm, to keep his wits sharp. There was no good to be had in letting himself think of this battle as more difficult than any other. Though that last thought proved near unbelievable, as the stomping in the stands and the roar of the crowd echoed in the holding pen. Asur stood alone on the ramp leading to the arena gate, only the grizzled doctore watched him from the shadows below.

The gladiator was a relative newcomer to the games of Rome, having started as a provincial fighter in the arenas of Judea and Egypt. In his youth, Asur had been a stable tender, though an uprising against Roman rule had seen a punitive expedition bring harsh justice upon the city. In the madness of reprisals, Asur had been captured and enslaved. He was lucky to avoid being sentenced to the mines, his skills with horse and mule saving him from such a bleak fate. For several years, the boy Asur had served as a stable slave, until such time as he'd grown to be a young man.

One day, without warning, after Asur had finished his morning chores, rough-handed mercenaries appeared in the

stable, took him in arms and led him
away. They told him he had been sold,
that he belonged to a different master
now. His new dominus was the owner of a
traveling slave caravan, they said, and
was in need of a strong young man to tend
his horses. And so it seemed Asur would
be given to a new life of travel. But
soon after, while out on the road, his
new master's camp was attacked by
raiders. Asur had unfortunately
distinguished himself by deftly cutting
down many of the men in a battle of crude
blades and fists. His new dominus took
note of this performance and was so
impressed with the ferocity of the young
man that he sold him to a lanista in
Judea the following week. The young man
would spend his next years as an arena
fighter there, hardening and perfecting
his brutal craft.

    "I am a long way from the bloody
pits of Judea and Egypt," thought Asur as
he ruminated on his past exploits. There
they had taught him to fight with sword
and spear, though because of his Thracian
blood, he was naturally chosen to fight
in the Thracian gladiator style. He was
shown how to fight with honor, how to
kill upon command, and how to wield the
shield and sickle sword of the Thracian
with deadly skill. Soon enough, the tales
of the new golem fighters in Rome reached
the ears of his dominus who sold Asur to
Lanista Laeca right away.

    Asur quickly discovered the radical
differences between life as a provincial

gladiator and that of a fighter in the
capitol of the empire itself. He found he
rather enjoyed the creature comforts,
being oiled and bathed, as much hearty
food as he liked, and the tender
attentions of women. He told himself that
nothing better could be hoped for by a
meager slave, and that glory and death in
the arena were small prices to be paid
for this life of luxury. Asur, who had
labored all his life, was unbothered by
the regimented and often grueling
training, as a hard life was a hard life,
and he could do little to change that. He
had been a slave for nearly all his
years; if not a slave to the Romans, a
slave to someone else.

Here in Rome, the whim of the crowd
often determined if a man lived or died,
unlike in the provinces where it was the
editor who decided. He knew the editor's
power in Rome was in title only, that it
was the mob of the populace who truly
ruled these arena sands. While not
handsome or charming, Asur was a good
gladiator and fought with skill and
honor. He may not have had the love of
the crowd, but in his time fighting the
golems of House Laeca, he had at least
earned the people's respect.

In the few months since being
purchased by Lanista Laeca, Asur had
fought four times in the arena against
the golems, sometimes in matched pairs
and once in a mass battle against a vast
horde. Though Asur knew he was slated to
fight a duel with another living

gladiator today, who could know what additional horror awaited him? It was something awful and spectacular dreamt up by the ever-increasingly cruel imagination of Lanista Laeca, no doubt. In preparation, he bowed his head and sent a whispered prayer to the gods of his fathers as the gates of the arena creaked open.

The Thracian stepped out into the arena where he was greeted with cheers and applause, many in the crowd chanting his name. On the other side of the arena stood the gladiator Prax, also of Ludus Laeca, who fought in the dimacheri style, a razor sharp gladius in each hand. The two gladiators walked towards the center of the arena, each basking in the applause of the crowd. Asur noticed that an equal number of voices chanted the name of Prax as they did Asur, such was the reputation of the dimacherus. While neither were champions, they had both been awarded the secundus bout and both had gained position. House Laeca was certainly on the rise, though it was on the backs of gladiators and golems as much as it was on the wit and savvy of Lanista Laeca.

Prax and Asur squared off with several paces between them, as was the custom. They turned to face the editor, holding their blades aloft in salute. Then, as the editor called for the match to commence, the gladiators began to circle one another. Prax was the first to strike, feinting to the left then lashing out with both blades. But Asur was a keen gladiator, and brought his shield up to block just as swiftly. Asur sent a counter-strike towards Prax's head, not expecting it to land, but forcing Prax to step backwards allowing Asur to gain momentum. Asur pressed the assault, driving Prax backwards with a flurry of blows from his sickle sword.

Through the flash of blades, Asur saw his opening and swung his shield low, connecting with Prax's ribs and hearing a satisfying crunch of bone as the blow sent the other man reeling. The dimacherus tucked his shoulder and rolled across the sand, using the momentum of the blow to carry him away from the Thracian and giving the gladiator time to spring to his feet, bringing his swords up for defense. The crowd had been cheering as battle was joined, but now their cheers turned to howls of delight, and both gladiators paused for a moment to observe the reason.

Low moans sounded and from both of the main arena gates came several golems, five by Asur's quick count. It was clear the gladiators were meant to fight amidst additional enemies, and neither paused for longer than a moment before rejoining the bout. Prax, having had a chance to catch his breath, lunged forward with his right gladius, which Asur turned aside with his shield. Then, with a fluid grace, Prax lunged and stepped forward with his left gladius, which Asur parried with his sickle sword. Prax had managed to engage both Asur's shield and sword with his own, and so unleashed a powerful stomp kick to the Thracian's chest.

Asur flew backwards and landed in a heap upon the arena floor. Prax closed the distance and just barely missed a downward stab into Asur's neck as the Thracian brought his shield up for a hasty block. Prax then spun away as he turned his two swords toward the grisly task of butchering a golem that had managed to reach them. Asur rolled away from the bloodshed and got to his feet just in time to shield-bash another golem that attempted to tackle him. The Thracian's sickle sword took off the top of the golem's skull, revealing the ruined brains within as it slumped to the ground.

Asur pulled his shield around his left flank, sending an attack, and caught the edge of Prax's gladius before it sank into his calf. The Thracian took several wild swings with his sickle sword, only to have them all parried by the dimacheri's spinning blades. Prax turned Asur's blade a fourth time and landed a solid slash across Asur's shoulder, cleaving away pieces of armor and drawing blood. As if the blood called to them, several more golems closed distance at a quickened pace, and the two gladiators broke apart to engage the new threat.

Prax danced out of the way of two golems as they rushed him, raking his swords across the back of one and knocking it over with the force of his strike. The dimacherus was a flurry of iron as he cut away both hands of the next golem, then opened its throat with another strike, finishing it off with a mighty thrust through the open wound and into its brain. As the dimacherus recovered his sword, Asur, with the gore of another golem sprayed across his torso, exploded from his right side and sunk his sickle sword into Prax's arm. The dimacherus yelled in pain and dropped his right gladius, but he held his ground and swept his back leg outwards, landing a second solid blow upon Asur's already injured shoulder. Asur dropped his sickle sword and staggered, the blood flowing freely from his injured arm. As Prax moved in for a killing blow, Asur dipped into a crouch and launched a powerful shield-bash into Prax's midsection that sent the dimacherus flying through the air, landing in a heap several steps away.

Asur saw the golem with the slashes on its back slowly rising to its feet and rammed his armored knee into its jaw. The golem fell onto its back as the gladiator raised his shield above his head and brought it down onto the golem's throat several times until its head separated from its body. Asur then threw down his shield and picked up the gladius that Prax had dropped. By then, the dimacherus had regained his footing and, with no golems left on the field, began attacking Asur again. While Asur was not a left-handed swordsman, the dimacherus had been

trained to fight with both hands, and
after several blows had been exchanged,
the superior skill of the dimacherus was
telling.

Asur fought as best he could, though
for every strike he parried, another
found purchase in his flesh, and none of
his own attacks got through Prax's
defense. Soon Asur was bleeding from many
wounds, and finally collapsed to his
knees. Without speaking, the Thracian
raised his two fingers to the sky, a
hand-signal used for pleading mercy from
the editor. Prax stayed his hand and
waited, while the crowd shouted for
death. The editor, swayed by the braying
of the people, made the gesture
signifying that Asur would not find mercy
in the arena today.

Asur closed his eyes and saw the
green fields of his youth, filled with
horses and bathed in yellow light, as
Prax drove the point of his gladius into
the Thracian's neck, downwards into his
heart.

THE HOPLOMACHUS & MURMILLO

At last, thought Bricius, a primus bout. The heavily muscled gladiator had long dreamt of this moment, though, truth be told, he never expected to see such creatures as the golems that stood in the arena. Bricius had grown up in the shadow of the Coliseum, born into slavery as the son of a gladiator in House Ursa. His father, Pwyll, had been captured during one of the many wars fought in Gaul, a region of the empire that needed constant quelling. Pwyll had taken well to the life of a gladiator, being a hard and pragmatic man, and had found ways to make peace with his fate. The former warrior fought his best and in time was granted privilege to marry and sire a child.

Bricius thought little of freedom, as he had been born into slavery and knew no other life. As a boy, he attended his father and the other gladiators during their training. He fetched water, bound their wounds, oiled and polished their weapons, and learned the lore of the arena from the voices of the men who lived and died upon its sands. The boy learned to value honor and glory, to protect his brothers and yet still hold ability to slay them in the arena when called upon to do so.

"There is a freedom in being a gladiator," his father used to say. "For us there are no nations, or gods, or gold. We fight because we must, for no cause beyond glory, and so the victories we win in the arena are pure, and belong to us. We are the heroic dead, my son. We are gods who walk among the living for a short time, and when we leave this world it is an honorable thing. The arena is a good place to die."

Bricius took a deep breath as he stood on the ramp leading to the arena gate next to his opponent, Agathias, the spear-wielding hoplomachus. Bricius fought in the Murmillo style, carrying a gladius and a large rectangular shield, and wearing a helmet with a fish crest. Typically, the murmillo fought the retiarius, for it was only natural that the fish fight the net, though for the primus, exceptions were made. Bricius had distinguished himself in the arena many times over, first as a provocatore fighter in House Ursa, fighting with blunted swords against other provocatore to get the crowd excited for upcoming bouts. Then, as his skills became more honed, and, as he grew from a youth into a man, he was purchased by Lanista Laeca.

Pwyll had died some years prior, falling before the sword of a secutor knows as Black Hand. It was at Pwyll's funeral that Lanista Ursa told Bricius that he would train to take his father's place. On that very night, the Black Hand and his dominus attended the funeral, and the Hand told the boy that his father had fought well. Bricius learned in that moment the true bonds between the gladiator brotherhood: that no man died alone, for his brothers all stood with him, in life and in death.

Bricius thought of this as he looked over at Agathias, resplendent in his polish armor with several ribbons of red tied upon his arms, legs, and spear. The hoplomachus insisted that it was all just theatrics, and the crowd did seem to appreciate the spearman's sense of flair; however, Bricius knew better, as the ribbons also served as a distraction to the man's opponents. The murmillo had never liked the flamboyant hoplomachus, though he did respect the gladiator's skill with a spear. Agathias had come to the ludus several years past, already a distinguished gladiator in the provinces. Lanista Laeca had thought wisely to bolster his ranks of recruits with gladiators who had already been blooded in lesser arenas.

Bricius and Agathias had been at odds with each other from the start. The murmillo was deeply committed to the lifestyle of the gladiator and was a believer in the glory of the arena. While the hoplomachus seemed to care little for discipline or honor, his tastes lying far more in the realm of rutting with women and drinking wine. The other gladiators, even old bloody Heraus, all favored Agathias, and he was well loved by the crowd. Perhaps it was his casual manner or his perpetual smirk that tested Bricius so. Perhaps it was that they had such different ways of being gladiators, he thought. He was a man who fought with determination and implacable endurance, and Agathias, a man who pranced and posed just as much as he fought.

Agathias noticed Bricius's gaze upon him and spoke, "If ever there were two champions in House Laeca, it would be us, brother. We have the primus."

Bricius nodded grimly, "There will be no quarter today hoplomachus, a house can have only one champion. I've seen little in the way of mercy in those primus I have born witness too."

Agathias threw his head back in laughter, startling the arena tenders who crewed the wench, making them step back warily. "Ever on the offensive, Bricius! Even beneath the arena you fight with words when swords are not yet drawn!"

Bricius bristled at that remark, then, as he saw no malice in the eyes of the hoplomachus, began to calm himself. "I have waited for this moment all my life Agathias, and, as one of us shall die today, perhaps I seek only to remain focused on the task at hand."

"Once we step onto those sands we shall be like the Titans of legend, and it will be glorious," smiled Agathias as he fastened his helmet, "If ever a man must fight another, the primus is surely the greatest of contests."

The platform began to move upwards, and Bricius spoke as he brought his own helmet down upon his head, "Well said, hoplomachus."

The gate to the arena opened, and the two champions emerged to the roar of

the crowd. Some chanted the name
Agathias, and others chanted Bricius. The
editor spoke with a booming voice,
calling out the great deeds done by each
gladiator, painting a picture of two
champions fated to do battle in the
primus. At the center of the arena, a
great ziggurat had been built, shaped
like a terraced pyramid and standing
nearly thirty feet tall. It had been
constructed of wood and stone, and in
several places on each terrace level was
a short flight of stairs that led to the
next terrace level. The top of the
ziggurat was flat, and an eagle banner of
Rome had been set in the stone. The first
gladiator to free the banner from its
setting was the victor, and the other, if
he still lived, would be put to death.

Agathias was escorted to one side of
the arena and Bricius to the other, as
over twenty golem gladiators were
released onto the sands. With the
champions in place, the editor gave the
call for the game to begin and the battle
was at hand. Bricius felt as if his blood
was on fire, this remarkable fight was
the moment his entire life had been
building towards. He reveled in it. The
murmillo sprinted across the arena floor,
sweeping the head off of the first golem
as he ran past it without pausing. He was
already several paces away by the time
the body hit the ground.

Bricius knocked another golem aside
with his shield as he advanced towards
the pyramid, and then another as he

parried the golem's sword and upper cut
the creature with his shield, its head
lolling as its neck snapped. The
gladiator kept his pace and continued
towards the ziggurat, reaching it in
several bounding steps. He slowed when he
realized with no small amount of shock
that the golem gladiator in front of him
was the retiarius Octavian. The murmillo
parried a surprisingly powerful thrust
from the golem gladiator, then
sidestepped the trident and sunk his
gladius into the creature's chest.
Bricius had to move quickly to bash the
golem with his shield before the creature
could bring its trident around for
another lunge. The murmillo could have
kept moving up the pyramid in that
moment, but chose to finish off the golem
gladiator who had once been one of his
brethren. "Stand with my brothers, in
life and in death," he whispered to
himself as he squared off with the undead
Octavian.

Agathias was visible for a moment as
he cleared the first terrace of the
ziggurat and moved on to the second.
Moments later, Bricius hugged the wall as
a golem came falling through the air from
above. It landed on the ground one level
below Bricius, its skull cleanly
punctured by what could only have been a
hoplomachus spear. Bricius had little
time to think on it, as he was attacked
by a large golem gladiator that wielded a
heavy maul. The blow knocked Bricius off
balance, his shield nearly flying from

his grasp. But the murmillo was a champion for no small reason, and he let the momentum of the blow carry him into a crouching spin as he slashed the legs out from under the golem, then drove the point of his sword into its skull in a series of fluid movements that garnered thunderous applause from the crowd.

Somewhere above, Agathias screamed, and for a moment Bricius feared the man had been killed by a golem. The thought saddened him as the hoplomachus, flamboyant though he might be, deserved to die at the hands of a fellow champion. Bricius pumped his legs and sprinted around the terrace level, knocking a golem off the pyramid as he moved along, sending the creature plummeting. He moved up the stairs and caught sight of Agathias locked in battle with another gladiator golem. The creature had sword and shield, and, despite its clumsy movements, had managed to slow the hoplomachus in his ascent of the ziggurat.

By the time Bricius reached the terrace just below the summit, Agathias came around the other side. He had just dealt the golem gladiator a deathblow, sending its corpse rolling down the shallow staircase into the massing horde below. "Good to see you at the summit, brother! Shall we commence upon one another or dispatch these golems first?" asked the good-humored hoplomachus as the grim murmillo looked at the eleven creatures swarming up the ziggurat.

"I would have proper contest, Agathias. Let us slay these golems!" shouted Bricius as he saluted Agathias with his sword. The salute was returned by spear, and the two men remained on opposite ends of the summit, keeping with the sport of the event; not overtly working together, but not yet attacking each other. Bricius and Agathias defended the summit against the eleven golem gladiators as the creatures rose to meet them, sometimes in pairs and sometimes alone. The crowd was howling with bloodlust and delight as the gladiators stood like Titans upon the ziggurat and cast down the golems as they came. Soon the last of the creatures toppled over the side as Bricius kicked its body and wrenched his swords from its skull.

The two gladiators, breathing heavily and pouring with sweat, began to circle each other at the summit, both consummate showmen, allowing the crowd to howl their praise as they drew out the tension. Bricius held focus on his opponent, not wanting to draw attention to the bite which now oozed blood from his left arm. He was so covered with gore that it was difficult for the crowd to notice the wound, but it did not escape the attention of Agathias, who met the murmillo's eyes with pity in his own.

"I'm done for Agathias, even if I win here, soon I'll be a golem just the same. It is a shame we must both die today, the games will be poorer for it," said the murmillo as he circled his enemy.

"Then let us embrace. The arena is a good place to die, is it not?" smiled the hoplomachus as he readied his spear.

"It is."

With that, battle was joined as the champions surged towards one another, deadly weapons whirling. Their contest was worthy of tale and song, two skilled warriors in their prime. The murmillo fighting stoutly with shield and sword as the hoplomachus moved in circles, constantly lunging with spear. Bricius stood resolute behind his shield, using it to deflect a flurry of spear thrusts then rushing in with his gladius for repeated attempts at stabbing the other gladiator's mid-section. Agathias cleanly blocked all of the murmillo's stabs with his small buckler, then swiftly changed his stance and swung the spear in a wide arc at the other man's legs.

A moment too late, Bricius realized the spear had been a ploy to draw his sword into a parry, and the hoplomachus smashed his buckler into the side of the murmillo's helmet. Bricius reeled from the blow, nearly losing his footing, and that was when he saw the hoplomachus gather his legs beneath him. Bricius knew the thrust was coming and started to move his shield into position, but a moment to late. The spear thudded into his chest.

His form was perfect, Bricius thought hazily as he began to sway heavily towards the edge of the summit.

The murmillo's heart was cleanly transfixed, his body outstretched and leaning backwards. As Agathias pulled on the spear, Bricius was released, and toppled over the edge. The gladiator's corpse tumbled down the ziggurat, landing in a pile alongside the many slain golems below. Before pulling the eagle banner from its setting, the hoplomachus paused to hold his bloody spear aloft in salute to the fallen murmillo. The arena was indeed a good place to die.

THE ESSEDARI

He had been a druid once, in the days when his name had been Maedoc, when his family lived under a roof built by his own hands, and his gods spoke to him with voices of wind, root, and hoof. He spoke the tree language, and he wore the white robes on feast days. Then the Romans came to the Green Isle, and they cared only for gold and slaves. They knew nothing of the gods. Their red armies had always stayed in Pictland, and the folk of the island were unprepared for the onslaught.

Maedoc's family had been put to the sword in the first days of a war that seemed unending. Like the Picts, the island folk were a hardy race and not suited to life under the iron rule of the Roman. Maedoc walked among the villages and raised many swords to his banner, and a mighty revolt they fought. Yet for every Roman slain, another took his place, and soon the rebel strength was spent and Maedoc himself was captured.

He had been tortured; the last of his men were executed before him, and the few women of his band were raped unto death while his eyes were forced open. Such was the reprisal of the Romans, such was the price of revolt. Maedoc was stripped of his name and given a Roman name to mock his revolt. So it was that Maedoc the Druid became Cassius Rex, or King Cassius.

Word of his skill at the reins of a war chariot had passed from legionnaire to slave trader, and slave trader to potential buyers. Soon Cassius Rex was forced, by brand and by lash, to race in the arena. He was so far from home that the voices of his gods were at first faint, and then silent. In time he learned to accept his life as one of the essedari, the chariot gladiators of Rome.

Only the wealthiest of Romans could sponsor games that involved spectacles of the essedari, as they required horses, chariots, and arenas large enough to provide the chariots room to move. As such, Cassius Rex soon found himself competing in the Coliseum of Rome. The former druid took what pleasure he could in this new life, becoming a friend to horses and nurturing a love for the speed of the wheel and the thrill of victory. Cassius Rex was an expert at the races, and also a master of spear and bow.

When House Laeca revealed the golems in the Coliseum, Cassius had felt the stirrings of old voices in his spirit. It was as if seeing the creatures had shaken him to his core, and at once he knew these were abominations of ancient magic and vengeance. He knew not what tribe had called down this curse, though a curse he knew it was. Leave it to the Romans to bring such a thing to the capitol of the empire and put it on display, he had thought. They are, in their own way, like me, a relic of some distant land that only exists in stories and the arena.

Lanista Laeca had made purchase of Cassius Rex some months later, once the lanista's wealth had begun to grow by leaps and bounds as his golem gladiators became the vice of the empire. Dignitaries and politicians flocked from everywhere to witness the creatures in the arena, while merchants and paupers alike flooded the city streets. As Lanista Laeca's power and influence grew, he promised the people of Rome a great spectacle of golems, gladiators, and glorious carnage unlike any other.

So it was that Cassisus Rex found himself in the Coliseum today, the crowd packed in like cattle, with the overflow leading well outside the viewing area. The editor had placed criers outside the arena to tell the tale of what happened inside, so those unlucky hundreds who could not witness with their own eyes could hear the deeds of the day. The sun was nearing the end of its course through the sky, and the shadows were growing long. Torches had been lit across the building, and many burned on long poles set in the arena floor.

Large stone pillars had been set in several places in the arena, serving as markers that would allow both the essedari and the crowd to follow the progress of the race. The arena was teeming with golems, many of which were the dozens of gladiators who had been slain during the last two days of games. There had to have been nearly half a century of golems and golem gladiators milling about the arena. A large canvas banner had been hung behind the editor's podium where the names of the six essedari had been written. The editor explained to the crowd that for every golem slain, the essedari responsible would receive a mark; for every opposing essedari slain, two marks; and for every lap he completed, he would receive three marks. They would race until all of the golems had been slain, and the essedari with the most marks would be awarded a rudius. To be awarded the wooden sword of freedom was to be set free from one's life as a slave, often accompanied by enough coin to start a new life as a free man. Those essedari who survived the race and yet lost the battle of marks, would be executed. Only one man would survive the day.

Cassius steadied himself and whispered soothing words to his horses, even as he worked to keep himself calm. The chance of freedom had ignited a fire within his spirit, a dream he had so long forgotten now awakened in him like a beast straining against the confines of his cage. He gripped the reins and looked down at his weapons rack. Within his chariot there was a short bow and several arrows, two throwing spears, and, fastened to the side of his chariot, his small oval shield. At his waist hung a gladius. Cassius, like the rest of the essedari, was very lightly armored, only having wrapped leather greaves on his calves, a heavy leather girdle to protect his belly and kidneys, and cloth wraps on his hands for holding the reins. The essedari had all dispensed with their helmets; though they had less protection, the editor had demanded it so that he could better see who performed what deeds.

The editor, his explanations now done, stepped back and called for the start of the race. Horns resounded and the essedari cracked their whips, sending the six chariots careening into the arena. Cassius held his reins in his left hand, using his right to crack his whip over the heads of the horses to drive them onwards. The golems had only barely turned towards the essedari when the six chariots slammed into their ranks.

Each of the chariots were equipped with long curved blades that protruded from the wheels on either side, and these blades scythed through the golems as if they were stalks of wheat. Most of the golems hit by the blades were taken in the legs, though some were decapitated as more chariots swept past them. The editor kept a careful watch and made marks for kills as they were made.

Cassius preferred to win races by keeping a steady pace and not using the limited energy of his horses on the first laps. He moved his whip to his left hand, which already held to the reins, and grasped a spear from the rack. The gladiator hefted the weapon into a throwing position, then using his left hand, tugged on the reins, veering his horses to the right and closing distance with the essedari nearest him. The other gladiator was too busy focusing on the chariot in front of him to notice Cassius closing in and hurling the spear. A cry went up from the audience as the spear burst through the essedari's chest and he fell from the chariot. The man's hands still gripped the reins, and it brought the horses up short, causing the chariot to flip back over front, crashing into the horses that had once pulled it.

Cassius veered left to avoid the crash and brought his whip across his own horses, spurring them onwards to complete the first lap. That was five marks for him within moments, and he was sure that he had scythed several golems with his chariot over the course of the race so far, though he dared not glance at the canvas to see how the others were doing. The screams of the horses filled the arena as the golems fell upon them, feeding on the fallen beasts as ravenously as they would the flesh of men. One arrow thudded into his chariot, then a second, as another essedari drew near Cassius. The former druid looped his reins on the pommel of the chariot and swiftly took up his own bow, notching an arrow as fast as he could. Both of the essedari were gambling that their horses would follow the track and not wreck the chariot while they used their bows. Cassius let fly with his own arrow, only to miss his target by mere inches. The enemy essedari loosed a second arrow,

this time into the flank of the right
horse that pulled Cassius' chariot.

The horse screamed and kicked, but
held its course. The crowd was booing
loudly, calling down curses on the enemy
essedari for his dishonorable shot,
though cheered even more loudly as
Cassius drew back another arrow. He let
out his breath in measured bursts as his
perception of the world slowed to a
snail's pace. Cassius placed all of his
focus upon target and arrow, pushing all
other details out of his mind, and then
let loose. The arrow flew true and
slammed into the throat of the enemy
essedari, who slumped out of sight.

Cassius discarded his bow, letting
it fall away as he grasped the reins
again, correcting the horse's path. The
horses had strayed from the course, and
Cassius had to turn in a wide circle to
complete his next lap, though he could
not remember if it was his second or
third. As he came around, he got a wide
view of the arena: it was a tempest of
chariots, dust, gore, and golems. Many of
the golems had been shorn at the legs or
waist and were now crawling across the
arena sands, dragging themselves along on
their hands. One essedari had crashed his
chariot, but had recovered his sword and
shield. As Cassius brought his chariot
around, he watched the stranded essedari
slay several of the golems, though the
gladiator was soon dragged down by the
crawling golems and devoured.

Cassius thundered back onto the

track, crashing his chariot into that of another, their blades snapping off as each was caught in the spokes of the other's wheel. The two men immediately moved their whips to their off hands and began fighting. Cassius reached for his second spear, only to find that somewhere in the melee it had been lost. So he drew his sword, just barely twisting his torso out of the way of a thrust from the other gladiator's spear. Cassius had to lean out of the chariot to slash at his opponent, while the other gladiator tried to keep his distance and impale Cassius upon the spear. After a flurry of blows, the chariots rounded the corner, and both gladiators were forced to temporarily abandon their battle to guide their horses through the corner.

As they took the corner, a golem that had been cut in half managed to heft itself aboard the former druid's chariot. It clawed at his shoulder, digging furrows in the man's flesh. Cassius screamed and let go of the reins as he bashed at the golem with the pommel of his sword, the creature falling away and disappearing into the dust. Cassius grasped his shield and stepped down from the chariot as it slowed to a halt. The horse wounded by the arrow had finally worn out, and it collapsed on the ground in front of him.

Cassius looked around the arena and saw that only the one essedari he had been fighting was still racing. All of the rest had crashed or been killed, two of them by his own hand. Cassius knew he could not stop moving, as the arena was still crowded with golems, though all that remained were shorn and crawling. He dispatched two creatures that were near him as he moved directly into the path of the final essedari. Cassius knew that if he had any hope of victory he had to un-seat the essedari so he could not complete more laps and pull ahead in score. As the chariot drew near, the enemy essedari drew his spear back for a throw, and Cassius ran directly at the chariot.

At the last moment, the enemy essedari hurled his spear, and Cassius ducked underneath the shaft. Then, as the chariot passed by him, he leapt over the remaining scything blade. As soon as he landed he hurled his shield like a discus, and, at the short distance, it struck the lower back of the enemy essedari who toppled from the chariot. The crowd was howling its applause as Cassius started sprinting for the other end of the track. He did not look behind him as he heard the sound of the enemy essedari being consumed by the crawling mass of golems.

Cassius reached the other side of the track in time to seize the reins of the runaway chariot, taking it for himself. He then rode down the last of the golems, finishing the bout with a sizeable score in addition to being the sole survivor. The rudius he received that day was to be his mark of freedom to any Roman he crossed, for he was Cassius Rex the essedari. The coins of the winner's purse bought his passage to the distant Green Isle, where the voices of his gods called to him as Maedoc the druid.

THE MANEAD

The wine slid down her throat, burning sweetly as it made its way across her tongue. This was the rite, the act of worship, and only the first of many she would perform this day. Dionysus whispered within her soul, stoking the fires the wine had ignited, filling her with purpose and hardening her resolve. Her god was with her, and there was no dousing the fire set in her heart.

Hesta looked at herself one last time in the mirror-like surface of the water basin. No longer did she see the grim slave girl staring back at her. The face she looked upon now was beautiful and terrible, eyes afire and a wicked smile slyly hiding on the edges of her lips. It had been a long journey to this day, rich with lust and courage, the meat and drink of her chosen god, Dionysus, the outsider god, the wanderer of the way, a harbinger god who brought careful wisdom and wild passion in equal measure.

I am a maenad now mother, she thought, I walk in your footsteps. I worship with wine and blood and lust. In this madness I shall offer up the whole of Rome to Dionysus. Though my flesh be forfeit, I shall not die a slave.

Her course was set, and her plans already in motion. She thought on the events of the past months as she grasped a small piece of coal and used it to draw symbols upon her smooth skin. She wrote the names of her family long forgotten, and she wrote the names of fellow slaves, most dead and gone, others lost to the vastness of the empire.

Dionysus had long been the patron god of her family, and though the life of a slave had been rigid, she had kept her covenants in secret. As the Lanista Laeca slipped deeper into his own darkness, so had Hesta's spirit held closer the flame of her ancient faith. When the lanista had unveiled his golems in the arena, it was as if the coin and glory had doubled his desire for her, and his cruelty. Swollen with his newfound wealth and power, he had become a monster. Hesta and the other slave girls were abused and humiliated, though Atticus chose to slake himself upon Hesta more than any other, and it was she that he marked.

It was the mark that pushed her over the edge, the spark that ignited the fire of the maenad in her. Lanista Laeca had returned from the Coliseum after the brilliant victory of Cassius Rex, flushed with pride and desire. He'd forced her to drink cup after cup of wine, until she was intoxicated and unable to defend herself. It was then he attacked her, hurling her to the floor and climbing atop her as he ripped away her clothing. He savaged her as he took her, moaning and grasping as if he had become one of the golem creatures upon which he had built his new fortune. His nails dug furrows into her back as he thrust against her, and, at the moment of his end, he bit her on the shoulder.

It was not the bite of a lover, but the mauling of a beast. Atticus worked his teeth into her soft flesh and Hesta screamed. The lanista bit deeper and deeper, moving his jaws to tear her skin and sink into the meat of her shoulder. Even with a head full of wine, Hesta screamed in pain and thrashed against the lanista. Her resistance seemed to only inflame his passion and re-double his strength. He moaned like his golems as he chewed, her blood smearing across his face and all over the floor. She fought as best she could while on her stomach, but to no avail.

It was in that moment a still small voice spoke within her spirit. Through it all she found a retreat, a sanctuary in the euphoria of pain mixed with the numbing intoxication of the wine. She let herself go to that place, leaving her body behind and soaring with the god. She saw Rome burning, the scrabbling hands of golems tearing apart slave and dominus alike, and at the center of it all she saw herself.

Hesta stood before the statues of the empire, facing them down and holding before her the tattooed head of the golem primus. She had known of the golem primus, the severed and undying head the centurion had sold to the lanista. Slaves of the house whispered of hearing it moan, and some had accidentally overheard Lanista Laeca speaking to it as if it were a man. In her visions, she saw herself there, holding the golem primus up to the statues as if she herself was Perseus using the severed head of Medusa to do battle against the Kraken.

To you I shall offer up this sacrifice, Hesta spoke silently to herself as she ran her hand across the wicked scar left behind by the lanista's assault. She was marked now, as if she was one of the lanista's golems, a cruel jape of domination and power, his own attempt at owning her soul in addition to her flesh. No longer, she thought to herself, for now I belong to myself, and to my god. Her thoughts fell upon the unfolding plan as she took up her butcher's blade, stolen from the kitchens, and drank another mouthful of sacred wine.

Once Hesta had healed from the lanista's assault, she had begun to execute her scheme. Most of the slaves in the household knew of the golem primus, and how Lanista Laeca would use it to create golems for the arena. She also knew that Atticus often kept a handful of the creatures in the old noxii cages down in the bowels of the ludus. Her first task was to seduce one of the guards, which proved easy enough. Hesta had wondered if she would be nervous coupling with another man, as Atticus had been the only man she'd ever known, but she quickly discovered just how powerful she could be as a woman. The guard was like clay in her hands, easily molded to suit her needs and happy to lay with her.

Unlike Atticus, the guard was not cruel and his desires were simple and over quickly. The guard never noticed that in their passion, Hesta had stolen his key to the cells beneath the ludus. She knew the guard would not report the keys missing, for in doing so he would lose his position. Likely he would assume he'd lost them while coupling with the golem-marked slave girl, and would certainly not report that, given that Hesta was the lanista's favorite.

Over the next several weeks, Hesta carefully assembled the mixture of herbs and spices that were to be mixed into the sacred wine of the maenad. Without observing the proper rites, this sacrifice would have no significance, and so it had to be done with reverence. Once the sacred wine was prepared, Hesta had taken a hearty jar of it with her into the pens beneath the ludus during the dead of night. She padded silently to the cell in which Drust, the blue painted man whose gaze had always followed her when she attended the lanista, resided. In the past, Drust had frightened Hesta, his scars and tattoos making him seem monstrous, though now she knew monsters more often looked like respectable men until the doors were closed. Hesta opened the Pict's cell, and found him crouched in the corner, fully awake and ready to pounce.

She had come to him then, boldly striding towards him and taking his body in hers. He resisted but for a moment, his dismay at her unannounced appearance giving way to his lust for the lithe body under his hands. In the darkness of the cell they coupled, sharing the sacred wine, and coupling again. As they thrust against one another, Hesta whispered her plans into Drust's ear, telling him of the sacred wine of Dionysus, of her seduction of the guard and the key, of her plans to unleash the golems upon the city. She told him that on the following night she would bring the gladiators a chance at freedom, though they would have to fight for it. Their sacrament of lust spent, she took the empty wine jar and left the cell.

The sacred wine granted strength, speed, and visions. That is what the ancient faith taught, and Hesta felt as if the world of spirit and the world of flesh were about to tear each other apart. She could not tell where one began and the other ended, and that was how she knew it was time for the final act. Her blade was keen, a larger flat knife of the butcher's trade, designed to hack through joints and bone. The incense smoke curled upwards, spiraling in the candlelight as Hesta whispered her prayer and stood. Using lard, she rolled her hair into locks, anointing them with incense. Her skin was covered in the names of her honored dead, and her veins burned with the fire of sacred wine while her loins thrummed with lust.

She slid from her chamber, keeping silent and watchful, not wanting any guards or slaves to see her until the moment was right. She crept through the sleeping villa, careful to remain in shadow, using her knowledge of the household to avoid the scant few guards and slaves who walked the halls. Finally, she reached the lanista's office, and, as she suspected, there was light shining from the bottom of the door. She took a deep breath and walked inside the room.

Lanista Atticus Laeca was at his desk, pouring over ledgers with the golem primus resting on a small wooden mount at the edge of the desk. The golem's gag was no longer the strips of leather used by the centurion, but fine chains of iron and gold that wrapped around from its mouth to its forehead. Atticus did not notice her at first, as Hesta had made sure to rub small amounts of pig fat in the iron hinges of the door, using herbs and incense powder to mask the smell. The maenad was halfway across the room before Atticus looked up and started to rise from his seat. Before he could stand or speak a single word, Hesta slammed the cleaver down into the lanista's forehead, burying the blade deep in his skull.

The horrified Lanista Laeca fell back into his chair, his body twitching as he made the smallest of groans. In moments, he stopped moving at all. Hesta paused for a few seconds, looking directly into the eyes of the dead man, then began quietly searching his desk for the ludus gate key. While she had the key to the cells and the noxii cages, she needed to give Drust and the gladiators the gate key in order for her plan to work. Soon she found it, and strung it around her neck. She then took the lanista's jeweled gladius from its wall hanging and grasped the golem primus by the chains, pulling it from its mount.

Her heart was pounding in her breast as she left the office and made her way deeper into the household. She went into the sleeping chambers of each of the guards and paid house staff. She stood over them as they slept, putting the golem primus next to their throats, then removing the gag. As the golem bit into their soft throats, Hesta held her hand, wrapped in sturdy cloth, over the victim's mouths. She'd seen what happened to men in the arena who were killed by the golems, and knew the bitten men would rise again within moments. Hesta had just finished using the golem on the last of nearly a dozen sleeping people when she heard the first moaning of a rising victim. It had begun.

Hesta rushed down the stone steps to the side-entrance to the ludus, where she knew there would only be one guard. It was a full moon, so she did not need a lantern or candle to light her way, and somewhere in the back of her mind she suspected that Dionysus would have helped her see in the black regardless. She was a divine instrument on this night, and could not be halted.

The guard never had a moment to reach for his weapon, as Hesta's sword flashed in the moonlight a mere breath before it transfixed him. The man crumpled to the ground and Hesta unlocked the doors. This was the moment upon which the survival of the gladiators hinged. There were six armed men in the guardhouse that served as the barrier between the gladiator pens and the ludus training area. Through a side door in the guardhouse, there was an entrance to the arming room where all of the weapons and armor for both training and arena combat were stored. If the gladiators were to have any hope of surviving the wave of carnage that was about to break upon the city, they must take that room. Even with her god's aide, she knew better than to attack six hard men herself. They were the best of the Laeca guardsmen.

She waited, keeping her breath shallow as she used her legs to hold herself steady at the top of the hallway leading to the entrance where she'd killed the guard. Her legs were splayed out, bracing against the walls, allowing her to hoist herself towards the ceiling. When the guards came through they would move beneath her, and she would remain unnoticed. Hesta had to hope that the chaos erupting in the villa would reach the ears of the men in the guardhouse and draw off enough of them that she could best the few who remained.

After what seemed like an eternity, and as her limbs began to quake from effort, she heard a bell toll in the distance. It was a warning bell to be sure, but was not of the pitch and keen of the bell in House Laeca. It had to be one of the villa estates nearby; the golems must have already spread out from the Laeca villa, she thought. She had left the door open to help the sound carry, and the guards finally took notice. Four of the six men took up their weapons and rushed down the hall and out into the villa, shouting back to their comrades the fate of the door guard.

As she worked her way back down to the floor, she could hear the sounds of fighting outside, and she knew the golems would penetrate the ludus soon. She crouched near the entrance to the guardhouse and then began to sprint. She ran through the guardhouse and right past the two remaining men, one dropping his shield in surprise. They both shouted and gave chase as she careened down the tight passageway into the gladiator pens. Despite the shouts and pleas of the gladiators, she rushed past them and into another hallway that led towards the noxii cage, only glancing back long enough to see the two guards had recklessly followed.

Hesta reached the noxii cages and immediately began unlocking them. Thankfully, the golems were possessed only of the most basic intelligence, so for a few brief moments they did not open the cages. Moving as fast as she could, the maenad hefted herself upwards next to the door, with one foot upon a torch holder and one hand holding the hilt of the gladius as she plunged it into a cross beam. She used the opposing tension to hold herself steady, though immediately her limbs began to tremble from the tremendous effort.

Heedless of danger and focused on their quarry, the guards burst into the room, leaving just enough space for Hesta to leap down and close the door behind them. She shoved her ludus key into the crude lock and wrenched it, snapping the key in two and leaving the door jammed. She knew it wouldn't hold for long, but it would buy her the time she needed. As she rushed back up the hallway towards the gladiator pens, she could hear the hinges of the noxii cages creak as the golems within surged forward. The screams of the dying guards filled the passageway.

Hesta returned to the gladiator pens, unlocking them as she went. The maenad paused only briefly to lock eyes with Drust and smile before sprinting out the side entrance and leaving the gladiators to their fate.

THE BOAR

He had been a laborer in his village, a long time ago, in the deep forests of a land the Romans called Germania. He had been a naturally strong boy, and, when he grew old enough to be named, the elders called him Heraus, after the great boars of the forest. He quickly proved his worth to the tribe, as he could do the work of several men. Heraus plowed fields for crops, cut timber for longhouses, stacked stones for cairns, and dug ditches for defense. His hands and back were never idle, and as he became a young man, his bed was never cold for lack of a woman.

His world was destroyed on a cold morning in early spring. With the dawn came a runner and tales of war, his breath misting in the morning frost. The runner told the elders of a great red army marching across the world, burning the sacred trees and poaching the tribes of gold and women. A great war chief called the tribes, and the runner had come to find brave men to join the fight.

The elders were divided in their council, though in the end it was decided that ten men must go. The men of his tribe were not unaccustomed to battle, though were as yet untested against the shield and spear of the Roman. Heraus had never seen a Roman, but he knew of them from tale and song: small men from the

lands near the sea, who fought like
devils and worshipped an iron eagle. He
had never killed a man and was just
barely one himself, yet with the vigor
and courage of a youth, he pledged his
axe.

They had set out on foot that very
day and marched for nearly two days
before reaching a larger group of
warriors. For the next week they marched,
their numbers growing as more runners
brought groups of warriors to join them.
On the eve of battle, their army numbered
nearly two thousand men, and Heraus could
not imagine what foe could stand against
them. Then the horns rang out, and the
sound of the enemy approaching grew
louder.

Three legions of Roman soldiers
marched into the field before them, and
Heraus began to doubt his estimation of
the foe. Battle-cries were given voice,
horns were blown, and the two armies
collided. Heraus was near the middle of
the horde of warriors, though he could
hear the din and chaos of the fighting
ahead of him. In that moment, he felt
like a child among beasts and cursed
himself for a fool at having marched this
far only to die a coward. He prayed to
the boar god to give him strength, even
if only to die as a man, and his grip on
the axe tightened.

Soon the fighting reached him as the
disciplined legionaries cut through the
loose ranks of warriors, using their
numbers to divide the horde into smaller

groups. Heraus lashed out with his axe
and grunted with surprise as it cleaved
his opponent's shield and sank into the
man's neck. Heraus pulled his axe from
the dead man and used his momentum to
turn and bury the weapon in the skull of
another Roman directly behind him. The
boar god had been listening.

Heraus marveled at his own strength,
pulling his axe free and turning on the
balls his feet to swipe at the feet of
another foe. As the Roman toppled over,
blood spurting from his severed thigh,
Heraus lashed out with the blunt end of
his weapon to knock over another soldier.
Without pause, Heraus stepped towards the
fallen soldier and hacked into the man's
chest. A legionnaire lunged at the
warrior with his spear, though Heraus was
able to twist his torso at the last
moment, and the tip only grazed his
chest. The wound was minimal, but
invigorating, and Heraus felt as if the
world slowed to the pace of a dream. He
stepped forward, past the shaft of the
spear, and drove the flat top of his axe
into the soldier's face as if it were a
spade into rich earth.

He felt like the heroes of the
bard's song, and screamed in exultation
as he fought. Two more soldiers fell
beneath his axe, then a third, then a
fourth. So intent was he upon his killing
that Heraus did not notice the greater
battle was lost. The Romans had
successfully divided the host of warriors
into smaller groups, forcing them to

fight back to back, gradually boxing them in. Outnumbered and barred from escape, the warriors were faced with the choice of death or surrender.

Most of the warriors fought wildly to a bitter and bloody end, dying in their hundreds and taking as many Romans into death alongside them as they could. Some few did throw down their weapons to plea for mercy, and so were clapped in irons and led away to be slaves. Heraus noticed little, his mind focused only on the stroke and recovery of his axe. It was not until the first spear pierced his side that his momentum slowed. His hand quaked involuntarily and his axe fell to the ground. When he tried to bend and pick up his weapon, he collapsed to the ground unconscious, the multiple cuts and bruises he'd suffered finally wearing him down.

Heraus thought of that day so many years ago as he rolled his head, popping his neck while he flexed his shoulders, a small ritual he'd been doing before fights since his early days in the arena. It amused him that while standing here in the catacombs, bleeding from several vicious bite wounds and facing down untold numbers of golems, he was thinking of that day. The first true fight in what turned out to be a lifetime of battles. Fitting, he thought to himself, that his aging mind wandered to his first battle even as he raised his axe to fight his last.

Hesta, the beautiful Greek slave who

had once been so kind to them all, had saved them and condemned them in a single stroke. They were out of their pens and arming themselves, and yet the golems had been unleashed into the city, which meant no clean escape. In his youth, Heraus had seen the wild shamans when the gods were inside them, leaping madly through fire and slaying beasts with their bare hands. He knew what that sort of divine madness looked like, and it was upon her. He knew little of any gods that were not his own, but he understood that Hesta intended to make a grand sacrifice out of the city of Rome. She had given the gladiators a slim chance at escaping before they too became part of her offering.

Drust had told the men one by one of his night with Hesta, whispering to them during the day's training. While many were jealous of her loins, all had listened to what she intended. Most of the men had come to trust her, and those few who did not trusted those who did well enough to follow. When Hesta sprinted past their cells, the gladiators had yelled at the guards, spurring them onwards to their doom. Then, as Hesta unlocked their cells, the gladiators rushed for the arming room.

Heraus had chosen his axe without hesitation, and with good reason. Years ago he had awakened from the battlefield to the sight of a medicae. He was bewildered, and tried to move, only to discover that he had been strapped to the table. A Roman officer entered the room and explained to the wounded man that his prowess and ferocity in battle was unlike anything that he had seen. Heraus found his life spared, provided that he earn this mercy in the arena.

It had been hard at first to find that spark that had ignited on the battlefield, and the first few fights did not go well for Heraus. Soon he had been defeated several times, spared only because the Roman arena crowd typically did not favor the execution of unconscious gladiators. His ability to sustain wounds and recover from them soon became his claim to fame, and he was purchased at a discount by Lanista Felix Laeca.

"Heraus the Boar," he had said, "that shall be your new name. If all that you are good for is bleeding and surviving, then that is what you shall do."

To his shame Heraus had said, "Yes, Dominus."

"The Coliseum is a place of glory and honor, and you, Heraus, seem incapable of winning either. In the underbelly of our society there is another sort of arena, the pits of the noxii, the condemned. They say you earned mercy on the battlefield once and have ill-used it since that time. Perhaps in the slaughter of lesser men you shall find your calling, and I shall have return." Felix had said these words before consigning Heraus to the bloodbath that resulted.

With axe in hand, Heraus now joined with Drust, Agathias, and the others in the guardhouse. "The girl has left us with golems at our back and Rome at our front. It'll be butcher's work to get clear of the city." Heraus stated as he fastened the chinstrap of his helmet.

"She has left us with little hope to be sure, yet we have our arms and our wits, that seems chance enough." Agathias laughed as he hefted his spear, "Even with the speed at which the golem curse takes a man after death, there cannot be more than a few dozen of them out there."

"Aye, though Hesta shall have made more by now, and those yet more in turn. She means to wipe out Rome itself," said Drust. "The local garrisons, night patrols, and the guards of every house will be drawing sword this night."

Agathias moved up the stairs and looked out the entrance through the small eye slot, the gladiators having already barred the door from the inside. The hinges were already straining as several of the golems hurled themselves against it over and over, most of them reanimated house guards. "A hard fight at the start if we go this way, lads. I say we go with Hesta's plan and leave through the ludus main gate." he said as he re-joined his comrades, "We'll likely have to kill a few of Laeca's guards, though I imagine none of us would fail to enjoy that."

Heraus grunted in assent and began making his way back through the guardhouse and out to the courtyard of the main gate. Drust crouched at his side, the other two dozen gladiators waiting behind them. There were two archers on the rooftop and two men guarding the gate itself. "We've strength and surprise enough to take the two at the gate, though we'll have hell raining down on us from those archers." spat Heraus as he surveyed the yard. Drust nodded, and gestured back at Agathias.

The hoplomachus joined them and followed their silent gestures to the archers on the roof. Agathias nodded and whispered, "Drust, stay with me, and hand me another spear after my first throw."

The hoplomachus grasped his spear and boldly strode into the courtyard, followed by Drust, carrying a borrowed spear along with his own weapons. Without war cry or pretense, Agathias hurled his spear upwards, the deadly missile arcing over the low roof and slamming into the belly of an archer. As the first archer crumpled, the second turned to see the hoplomachus readying himself for another throw. Agathias gracefully stepped forward and this time let out a shout as he made his second throw. The spear flew wide, missing the archer by an arm's length; still the archer lost his footing in an ungainly attempt to dodge, and fell backwards down the other side of the roof and out of sight. Agathias looked back at Drust, who was frowning, and said "Close enough."

Heraus and the other two dozen gladiators filed out into the courtyard, quickly creating a wall of fighters, bristling with weapons and malice. The two gate guards, both standing with swords drawn, looked at the assembled gladiators with fear. Heraus stepped forward "We are leaving through those gates, boys, and little love is borne you by these good men assembled. Stand aside."

At the sight of Heraus the Boar who stood with more than twenty gladiators at his back, the two guards threw down their weapons at once and backed away from the gate. Drust strode forward and drove the point of his sword into the throat of the guard nearest him, and, as the other man turned to flee, the Pict closed the distance in a few bounds and skewered the guard through the back. Drust turned to his comrades, face grim and blood-spattered, his voice barely above a whisper, "The Picts have no word for mercy." Drust turned and used Hesta's gate key to turn the lock, and, with the help of two other gladiators, they pushed the gates of the ludus open to freedom and golems.

From there it had been a hard fight, Heraus later recalled, as the screaming horde of golems began to fill the catacomb corridors before him. The gladiators left the ludus as a unit, doing their best to watch each other's backs as they made their escape. One of the men, a tribesman named Prax, had been a stone hauler's slave before he'd been a gladiator, and had himself carried many of the stones that built the essedari annex of the ludus before catching the eye of the lanista. Prax led the group through the streets and away from the core of the chaos, though it seemed the golem plague had pulled ahead of them.

"Hesta must be heading for the center of the city," muttered Agathias, "transforming people as she goes. The woman shall be the death of us."

"What about the catacombs?" asked Qais, a Thracian who had once been a noxii, condemned to the pits before fighting his way into favor with Lanista Lacea as one of the few men who survived a fight with Heraus the Boar. "There are entrances all over the city. I used to know them, and many exits as well."

"I hear people get lost down there, never to be seen again." said Prax, "Do you know your way once inside?"

"If there is a way, he'll find it." grunted Heraus, "We must leave the open streets. Soon the legionaries will respond to the golem riots and we'll have both the eagle and the golem tearing at us."

The men nodded their approval, and Prax and Qais led them deeper into the city towards the catacombs. The men moved as quietly as they could, letting the screams and sounds of the growing golem plague mask their movements. Though, the creatures began to appear and attack them in larger and larger groups, making it a hard task for the group to remain unnoticed by the Romans.

Horns blew and alarm bells tolled as the city became a battlefield, the golem plague finally reaching its full momentum and washing across the city. The gladiators fought hard, gaining ground and moving through the streets as swiftly as they could without turning their backs to anything but a comrade. They were the finest golem fighters in the empire, and still they were pressed.

Finally, after a grueling and bloody march across a third of the city, they reached an entrance to the catacombs. Prax was dead, killed several blocks back, and he had not been the first. Of the twenty-six gladiators that escaped Ludus Laeca, only seventeen remained. The distance covered by the brotherhood of gladiators had been measured in the lives of nine men. Qais lifted a small metal grate, then without a word, crawled into what to all appearances seemed to be a hole in the street.

The other gladiators followed suit, and soon they were moving through the darkness of the catacombs, searching for an exit. The group wandered through the blackness for what seemed like hours, and for all accounts could have been. Sometimes they could hear the sounds of battle and chaos in the streets above, and if there had been any hope of the Romans throwing back the hungry tide, it seemed lost. For the gladiators, there was a grim sense of justice to it all, as the golems tore down the capitol of an empire that enslaved them all.

As if the obstacles set against them were not enough, their guide Qais was killed in a surprising golem attack. The creature had emerged from the darkness and torn out his throat before he could even react. As he collapsed in a bloody heap in front of the men, Drust leapt forward and plunged his dagger through the golem's eye socket, then side-stepped another as it rushed him, leaving another gladiator room to shield-bash it to the ground. Drust drove the point of his dagger into the fallen golem, as Heraus and Agathias stepped around him to slay several more of the creatures.

A low moan began to fill the catacombs, and in the darkness the men began to panic. Drust stood and spoke, with an iron edge to his voice, "We cannot lose the initiative, it is we who are on the attack. Keep moving, and we'll find a way out. And someone kill Qais, quickly."

Heraus chuckled at the memory of that, the pragmatism of the blue man had always amused him. The golems were closing in then, and soon they would reach him. The gladiators had moved and fought and moved and fought, until, when all seemed lost, they finally found an exit. It was a drainage tunnel that emptied into the river. The men would have to crawl down the small enclosure, no wider than a shield's breadth, then would emerge into open ground again. At least, that was the theory. They had no way of knowing for sure, though the general consensus was that it was worth a try.

By that time everyone in the group, which was now only six men, including Agathias, Drust, and Heraus, knew Heraus had been bitten several times. Neither they nor he could be sure when he'd sustained his first injury, so accustomed they all were to Heraus being wounded and impervious to the pain. "I cannot go with you my brothers, nor shall I bend to a mercy killing. I'll fight them here." he said gravely as the men began to strip off their armor, taking only breeches and blades for their journey into the tunnel.

"A hard place to meet death, my friend. Surely you would see sky before you meet your gods?" asked Agathias as he paused at the tunnel's entrance.

"A man must stand against them, here, long enough for the rest of us to make good our escape, else they would simply follow us. Eventually we would need rest, and they would be upon us." Drust said as he tied a cord around his dagger so that it could hang from his neck while he climbed.

"The Pict is right, Agathias, and I am already a dead man. Go find freedom and make use of it." said Heraus as he clapped his hand upon the hoplomachi's shoulder, then he turned his back on his brothers, and they climbed.

Now he stood, alone in the tunnel, as the golems surged towards him. His vision had begun to blur and his limbs felt weak with blood loss and fatigue.

Sometimes it felt as if the darkened tunnels of the catacombs were actually the snow-crusted forests of Germania. He shook his head, trying to clear the fog from his mind.

Lanista Felix said I once was shown mercy and made ill use of it, he thought, and I thought he was right. I sought to find my place in the pits of the noxii, wading in lakes of blood.

The first of the golems reached him, and he split its skull with a stroke from his axe. Then he pivoted on the balls of his feet and slammed the axe into the face of a Roman legionnaire who fell to the ground, spurting blood across the snow.

My place is here, he thought, in the last true fight. His axe struck home again, and another golem collapsed to the ground. The gladiator felt a sting on his leg, and looked to see that a Roman legionnaire had sliced his leg open. Heraus responded by caving in the Roman's helmet with the butt of the axe. The gladiator kept his momentum going, and stepped into a mighty stroke that cleaved another legionnaire in half at the waist, then with the back swing, decapitated a golem as it rushed in.

The snow was falling, and the gladiator wiped the blood from his eyes as the Romans closed in. He felled another golem, then a spear punctured his side, and he dropped his axe.

"And my god is with me."

Heraus fell to his knees as he grasped for the axe, then disappeared under the weight of several golems as they leapt upon him from all directions. As they ripped him apart, his last thought came clear to him: I am Heraus the Boar, and I do not need your mercy.

THE LEGACY

Centurion Cyprian Africanus died in his bed as an old man, survived by his son, Titus Africanus. Before the aged veteran breathed his last, a summons was sent to fetch his son. The young man, Titus, had followed in his father's footsteps and joined the legion. So great was the honor his father had won in the Servile War that the Legio VII had been re-formed. The legion was new yet, though had recently won its first honors during a punitive expedition against the Maedi tribes in northern Thrace.

When Legionnaire Titus received the summons, his centurion was happy to grant him furlough enough to make the journey home to attend his dying father. Included with the summons was a sealed scroll, with instructions for it to be broken and read by none other than Titus himself. It read as follows:

"My beloved son, long have I awaited news of your campaign and some weeks past I received word that the Legio VII had won honor in far Thrace. I am confident that you served bravely and with distinction, and I trust in the gods Mars that you survived your conflict and in Mercury that this message reach you.

I must tell you now that I am dying. The same wasting disease that took your mother seems to have found purchase in my own flesh, and I fear that I do not have much time left in this world. For that I am grateful. It has been a long and bloody journey, my son, and I shall welcome its end.

Do not think me macabre or possessed of an ill spirit, I am healthy in mind, if not in body. I am a man burdened by knowledge: there are certain truths that I must impart upon you, and because you are my son, these are soon to be your burdens to bear.

The Empire is full of secrets, Titus, and the men who keep them are as cunning as they are dangerous. I carry secrets, and am sworn to protect them upon penalty of not only my death, but of my family as well. My sweet wife has perished from this world, and my only son has now grown to be a good man and a fine soldier. These keepers of secrets cannot harm me any longer, and now it falls on you to bear my secrets, and make your own choice as to what you do with them.

As you know, I was with the Legio VII in its final days in Judea. We were suppressing rebels throughout the region, and we drove the last of the dissenters to a mountain fortress known as Masada. What you have been told, what everyone has been told, was that we met fierce resistance, and the legion sustained heavy losses taking the fortress. Then, the night of the siege, there was a massive rebel counter-attack, and though we emerged victorious, nearly two thirds of the legion were dead.

The truth, my son, is that we

angered the god of the Israelites and he sent a doom to walk among us. I discovered the first of the golems, the golem primus. It was a man made of clay and given life by the priest of the tribe. This golem bit the rebels, and they in turn attacked us, and soon we attacked each other. My fellow officers and myself worked hard to suppress knowledge of what happened to the legion, and our veterans were ordered to silence under the penalty of not only their deaths but that of their families.

But none of the men knew of the golem primus. The two legionnaires who went into the temple with me that morning were killed in the night's massacre. I was greedy, son. I was taken with a lust for coin, as if wealth beyond my soldier's pension would wash from my mind the horrors I'd witnessed.

I sold the golem primus to Lanista Atticus Laeca, whom you no doubt have heard of. By the gods but what great sport he gave in the Coliseum with his golems and his gladiators! Though terrible, it was also glorious was it not? To his credit, the lanista never revealed the golem primus and not a soul knew the secret of his creatures. Nor did they care, for it was only in the arena that the golems were seen.

The scribes write of the Servile War, and, as you know, it was during that war that myself and the other old soldiers were given a chance to prove our worth once more in battle. They write that a slave revolt engulfed the city. It offends me in my old age to read that good, hard Romans were massacred by slaves, as if the rabble could rise against us. There is even rumor that gladiators rose up, that good houses like that of Atticus Laeca were put to the sword by their own stock.

The truth of it is, Lanista Laeca was murdered. I do not know the details of his death, nor of the fall of his house, though I do know what I saw. We marched upon Rome, four legions swiftly mustered from the provinces, two of those mere recruits as yet untested in battle. For eight grueling days, we fought the golems, street by street and house by house. For every one of our men they killed, that man would rise as one of them, and so had to be fought and slain again.

Of the four legions we marched into the teeth of the battle with, there remained but one at the end of it. It was one of the greatest achievements of the Roman military ever to be won, and in my old age it sickens me to know that future generations will only ever read of this as a battle with slaves. Good men died, Roman men, defending the empire, and they deserve their place among the honored dead.

My greatest burden, Titus, beyond the truths I have revealed, is the golem primus. I found it, there in the dark heart of the city. A golem woman, so badly mauled that I could not divine her

age or nation, was at the head of a
mighty host of the golems. Her eyes
burned with the kind of hatred and hunger
that I'd only seen in the eyes of one
other golem, the rabbi himself who had
created the golem primus. She screamed at
us and attacked with a ferocity I'd still
not thought possible, even after
everything I'd seen.
As I was freeing my blade from her skull
I noticed that hanging from her belt was
the golem primus itself, and knew in an
instant that she must have been a slave
of House Laeca. Was she the reason the
golem plague had spread so quickly? I
cannot tell you with certainty, though I
suspect it, for how else would she have
the golem primus but to have wrested it
from the hands of Atticus Laeca himself?
He would not have parted with it
willingly.
    I have held the golem primus in
secret, here in our family villa. Do you
remember the old pagan cairn we found
while hunting? You were just a boy then,
but good with a bow as I recall. I hid a
strongbox in the cairn, and inside it
rests the golem primus. I have long
studied its secrets, and have come to
know the one way that the golem primus
can be destroyed. The tattoo on its
forehead is the Hebrew word for 'life'.
To destroy it, you must flay the skin of
the first letter from its forehead, thus
changing the word to 'death'. I have not
done this deed myself, Titus. Perhaps if
I were a stronger man, not grown so

sentimental in my age, I would have been able to destroy it. Alas that is not so, and now I am too weak to leave my bed. Thus, this legacy shall pass to you.

I brought this doom upon Rome, my son, for it was I who sold the golem primus to Lanista Atticus Laeca. Hence I go into my final days with peace in my heart, for a lifetime of horror and war is nearly over, and I shall be able to rest. For you Legionnaire Titus Africanus, so informed of the truth of many things, the shadows of life have grown darker. I know that you will make the right choice, my son, to use the golem primus as the mightiest of weapons, or to destroy it forever. If I am dead and gone by the time you reach me, know the choice is yours. I am sorry for the burden you now bear, but trust in your ability to take it on. Please forgive me."

As Titus neared his father's home, he drew his steed to a halt and looked in horror as smoke filled the sky. He spurred his horse onwards and rode into the burning villa. Bodies were everywhere, some of the house guards and slaves, others were the barbarians known as Visigoths.
Titus rode hard for the cairn, following the tracks of many warriors afoot. His worst fears were confirmed, as he neared the cairn and saw that it had been torn apart and plundered.

He dismounted and looked into the cairn, his eyes resting on an open strongbox covered in blood. As he stared, his hackles rose, and he spun around, sword in his hand. Before him stood a barbarian warrior, pale as death, with ragged bite wounds in several places on his body. Legionnaire Titus Africanus stepped boldly forward and swept the barbarian's head from his shoulders. The legionnaire then mounted his horse and swiftly followed the obvious path the Visigoth raiding party had taken.

It was several hours before he reached their camp, only to find it savaged and empty. It had all the signs of a great battle being fought. There were discarded weapons, overturned wagons, and smoldering cook fires left unattended. What held his horrified gaze, though, were the many mangled carcasses and disembodied limbs of what must have been Visigoth warriors. Then he noticed the large number of ruddy tracks leading away from camp. His breath caught in his chest at the terrible realization of what horror was unfolding.

The tracks were all heading south, towards Rome.

12833079R00073

Printed in Great Britain
by Amazon.co.uk, Ltd.,
Marston Gate.